SHREWSBURY & HEREFORD

DEDICATION

This volume is dedicated to my late wife Velda, who died in February 2005 after many years of illness. Being very much an English rose, she loved those parts of the country such as the counties in this volume, as the epitome of the sort of England she cherished. She was familiar with the railway operation in the area as she had been a senior secretary at Regional Headquarters, Paddington, where she had worked since 1948. In that time she aspired to working as secretary to several senior managers, and deputised for the general manager's and deputy's secretary. We married in 1971 and enjoyed many years of married life together until she gradually became more and more immobile with MS during the 1990s. She was always noted at Paddington (and Croydon where she worked for a while) for the immaculate layout of her work, and this shone through in other aspects of her abilities and in her appearance.

Designed by Paul Karau
Printed by Amadeus Press, Cleckheaton

Published by
WILD SWAN PUBLICATIONS LTD.
1-3 Hagbourne Road, Didcot, Oxon, OX11 8DP

THE NORTH & WEST ROUTE

VOLUME TWO

SHREWSBURY & HEREFORD

by
JOHN HODGE

WILD SWAN PUBLICATIONS

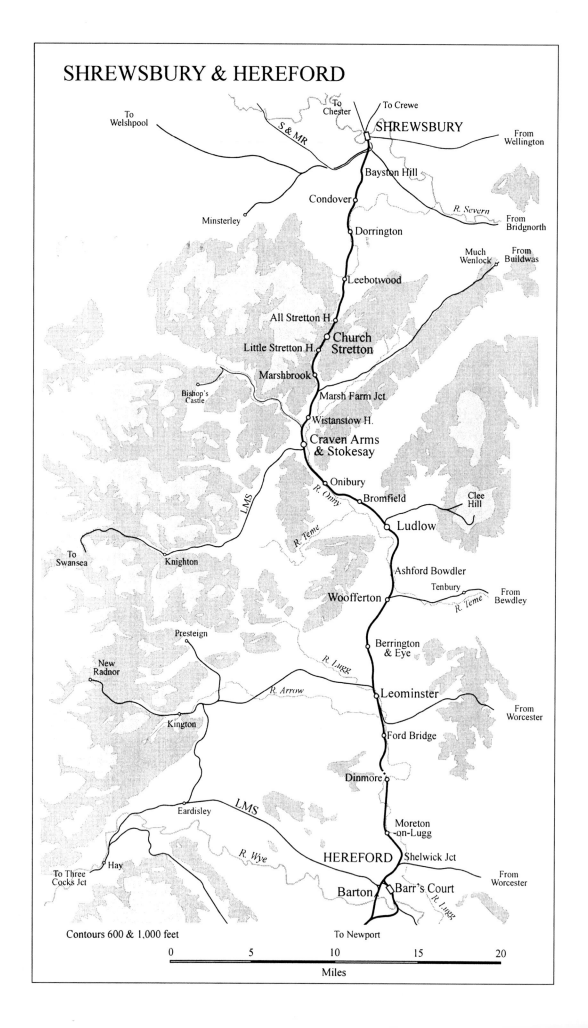

SHREWSBURY & HEREFORD

To Welshpool

S & MR

To Chester

To Crewe

SHREWSBURY

From Wellington

Bayston Hill

Condover

R. Severn

From Bridgnorth

Minsterley

Dorrington

Leebotwood

Much Wenlock

From Buildwas

All Stretton H.

Church Stretton

Little Stretton H.

Marshbrook

Bishop's Castle

Marsh Farm Jct

Wistanstow H.

Craven Arms & Stokesay

Onibury

R. Onny

Bromfield

Clee Hill

LMS

Ludlow

R. Teme

To Swansea

Knighton

Ashford Bowdler

Tenbury

From Bewdley

Woofferton

R. Teme

Presteign

Berrington & Eye

R. Lugg

New Radnor

Leominster

From Worcester

R. Arrow

Kington

Ford Bridge

Dinmore

Eardisley

LMS

Moreton -on-Lugg

R. Wye

Hay

HEREFORD

Shelwick Jct

From Worcester

To Three Cocks Jct

Barton

Barr's Court

R. Lugg

Contours 600 & 1,000 feet

To Newport

0   5   10   15   20

Miles

CONTENTS

FOREWORD

It seems incredible that the photographs in this volume were taken over 50 years ago. Like the first volume in this series on Shrewsbury itself, this book was inspired by the photographs of R.O. (Bob) Tuck who was a close friend at Cardiff since the mid-1950s. He used to attend business meetings at Shrewsbury where he took many excellent photographs from 1951, and began travelling to such meetings by car in order to be able to stop off at places along the route for railway photography. As such, he became one of the very few photographers ever to photograph the North and West line in its entirety between Shrewsbury and Newport. Though his photographs of intermediate places along the line were not many, I have managed to create a comprehensive coverage of each location, especially from the collections of Russell Mulford, Michael Mensing and Derek Cross, not forgetting the indomitable Henry Casserley – was there anywhere that man didn't photograph?

I hope this work recreates the atmosphere and brings back pleasant memories of the steam age along this important line, until the electrification of the West Coast Main Line in the 1960s robbed it of through express services between the North and West as they were transferred to run via Birmingham New Street and Gloucester en route from Crewe to Bristol. Now the line is populated by the fast new generation DMUs running from Manchester to Milford Haven (evoking memories of that other abortive attempt), but still often sees steam in the form of the preserved express passenger engines which run that way on special charters, and on which they can still show their capabilities.

The third volume in the series will deal with Hereford to Newport, but meanwhile, I hope you enjoy the memory of steam in this second part of the North and West series.

The station at Shrewsbury, probably seen here before the Great War, looking north. The presence of Great Western and London & North Western stock highlights its joint nature, with a L & NW service seen in the bay to the right, behind a small tender engine, possibly bound for the Stafford line. The prominent platform identification boards display the post-1904 numbering arrangement, whereby the station was extended southwards over the River Severn viaduct.

STEPHENSON LOCOMOTIVE SOCIETY

HISTORICAL INTRODUCTION

THE standard gauge North & West line existed as a route between the North of England and South Wales from 1854, though gauge differences prevented long-distance through running at that time. Between Shrewsbury and Coedygric (Pontypool), the line was built by two independent companies: the Shrewsbury & Hereford Railway, opened throughout in 1853 (initially Shrewsbury to Ludlow, in 1852), and the Newport. Abergavenny & Hereford Railway, opened in 1854. The final connection into Newport was provided at that time by the Monmouthshire Railway, and its station at Mill Street; a short road journey to or from the South Wales Railway's High Street station was necessary to travel beyond.

By the Act of 14th June 1860, the Newport, Abergavenny & Hereford company amalgamated with the Oxford, Worcester & Wolverhampton and the Worcester & Hereford Railways to form the West Midland Railway, and this in turn amalgamated with the Great Western Railway on 1st August 1863, in company with the South Wales Railway. The Shrewsbury & Hereford company remained independent until July 1870, when it was vested jointly in the Great Western and London & North Western Railways.

In 1874, the N&W line became a full through route with the completion of the Pontypool, Caerleon & Newport Railway, which allowed through running between Pontypool Road East and the South Wales Main Line at the Maindee Junctions, to the east of Newport station; this had been made possible with the conversion of the South Wales Main Line from broad to standard gauge during 1872. The PC&N company was vested in the GWR during July 1876.

The N&W line also became a through route between Shrewsbury and Bristol with the opening of the Severn Tunnel in 1886, though it was not until the final gauge conversion of 1892 that through rail traffic could travel beyond Exeter. It became an extremely important route, connecting the North of England with South Wales and the West Country, particularly with military traffic in times of war, and as a holiday route in peacetime.

PRE-RAILWAY TRANSPORTATION

A significant road connection between Shrewsbury and Hereford was effectively formed in Roman times, but the development of other roads in the area came much later as habitations were established beyond that immediate area. These were initially little more than footpaths, sufficient to carry a limited local foot and horse traffic, or perhaps driving small numbers of animals. As the use of wheeled traffic expanded in the middle ages, the road system became more akin to the system known today, connecting larger centres of population, and market towns with surrounding villages and hamlets. Their routes were also determined by other local factors such as ownership, terrain, and the need to cross rivers or other obstacles at suitable points. Shrewsbury and Hereford became focal points for both longer-distance and local road networks.

Rivers were also utilised for transportation, but were limited by their direction of travel and by natural obstacles, whilst the depths and currents varied by seasons.

By 1675, cartographer John Ogilvy had surveyed the Shrewsbury and Hereford route as a through way between Chester and Bristol. The road passed by way of Church Stretton, Onybury (Onibury), Ludlow, Lyston (Luston), Lemster (Leominster), and Dunmorehill.

A transport system that effectively made its appearance in the eighteenth century was the horse-drawn tramway, which required a significant amount of traffic to become feasible. Such tramways were thus mainly associated with mineral traffic, and a connection between Hereford and the Abergavenny area was finally made in 1829.

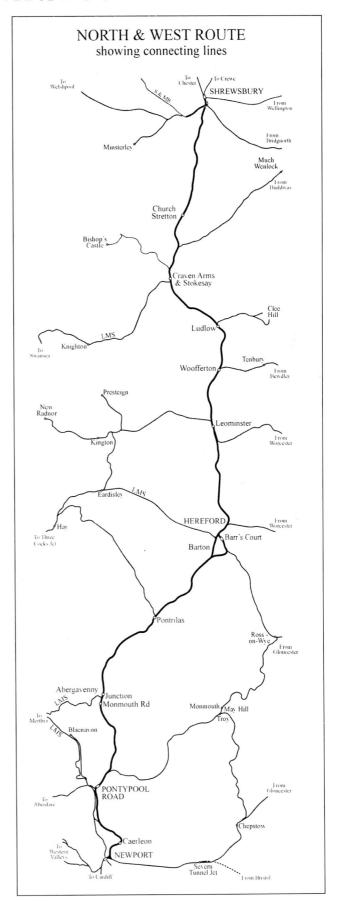

Canals were similarly established for bulk transportation, often connecting with a convenient river. Expensive to build, they could also suffer from many of the restrictions experienced in river navigation, particularly in maintaining water levels and crossing hilly terrain.

However, the rural and geographical aspects between Shrewsbury and Hereford permitted only road transportation. In 1830, the route was served daily by a Hereford & Chester coach, *Royal Mail*, in each direction. The approximate timings were:

Southbound

Shrewsbury	12.0 noon
Church Stretton	2.30 p.m.
Ludlow	4.45 p.m.
Leominster	6.0 p.m.
Hereford	7.30 p.m.

Northbound

Hereford	5.30 a.m.
Leominster	7.0 a.m.
Ludlow	8.35 a.m.
Church Stretton	11.0 a.m.
Shrewsbury	12.45 p.m.

Whilst these two coaches formed the 'express' services, carriers provided interconnecting 'local' movements for both basic passenger and freight traffic between the towns and villages, and at times also a much cheaper alternative over greater distances. For example, regular carriers left Shrewsbury on Saturday afternoons for Church Stretton; on Mondays, Thursdays and Fridays for Ludlow; and Tuesdays and Fridays for Leominster, serving intermediate points. From Hereford, regular carriers ran to Leominster on Wednesdays and Saturdays, and daily to Shrewsbury, all with balancing services.

However, the passage of these coaches and the many carriers who plied the route was often severely hampered by the state of the roads, particularly in the winter months.

The appearance of the railways was therefore seen as the panacea to all transport ills.

THE SHREWSBURY & HEREFORD RAILWAY

Main trunk routes of the railway system appeared around this area of England and Wales from the late 1840s. At Shrewsbury, the Shrewsbury & Chester arrived in October 1848, and the Shrewsbury & Birmingham in June 1849, the two later forming the northern section of the GWR's Northern Main Line. Both railways were built to the standard gauge. However, perhaps the most significant opening insofar as the North & West traffic was concerned was the Crewe line of the L&NWR, opened to Shrewsbury on 1st September 1858. A detailed account of the development of railways in the Shrewsbury area may be found in Volume One of this series.

In the south, the South Wales Railway was opened between Chepstow and Swansea on 19th June 1850, and was connected to the Great Western system a couple of years later. Other companies' lines were established in South Wales around this time, including the Monmouthshire Railway & Canal Company, whose line between Newport (Mill Street) and Pontypool (Crane Street) was opened in 1853.

To the east, Worcester was reached by the Oxford, Worcester and Wolverhampton Railway in October 1850 with its branch from the Midland Railway, whilst the main line between Oxford and Wolverhampton was completed by 1854.

The first significant attempt to provide a railway link between Shrewsbury and Hereford occurred in 1835/6 with a proposal for a Hereford, Shrewsbury & Grand Junction Railway; this was introduced around the same time as a Gloucester and Hereford scheme.

However, despite the initial excitement caused by the plan, support soon dropped away in this financially unstable period.

It was not until 1844 that the prospect of a railway connection was raised again, with a partial route given by a proposed Hereford, Leominster, Ludlow & Birmingham Railway. As with the previous scheme, the realities determined otherwise, and the idea was postponed.

In 1845, two more schemes were mooted. The first was a broad gauge railway, the Shrewsbury, Hereford & North Wales, with Brunel as its engineer; this was seen as an extension of another of Brunel's ongoing projects, the Monmouth & Hereford (Standish, Ross and Hereford). Although the Monmouth did receive approval, Brunel's scheme for a line between Hereford and Shrewsbury was not endorsed by Parliament.

The second scheme was for a standard gauge route, the Shrewsbury & Hereford Railway. This proposal subsequently changed its title to the Shrewsbury & Herefordshire when collaboration was envisaged with another intended concern, the Welsh Midland Railway (who had a similar route in mind), though when the Welsh Midland scheme was abandoned, the S&H company reverted to its original name. This scheme successfully cleared the many hurdles of the Parliamentary process, and the Shrewsbury & Hereford Railway Act was sanctioned on 3rd August 1846, involving Incorporation and permission to construct. The line formally ran from Coton Hill Jct. in Shrewsbury to Barrs Court Jct. South (a junction with the later Hereford, Ross & Gloucester company) at Hereford.

This railway, having a length of some 51 miles, was to climb southwards from Shrewsbury into higher ground around Church Stretton, then descended along the Quinny Brook and River Onny valleys into gentler lands around Ludlow, passing then to Leominster to follow the River Lugg on its way to Hereford. It was, in the main, a straightforward project, running as it did through countryside with relatively few significant obstacles to overcome, other than the tunnels required through higher ground at Ludlow and Dinmore, and at Shrewsbury (Coleham), where a 220-yard viaduct was required over the Rea Brook.

The promoters of the line were mostly the same people who had sponsored the Shrewsbury & Chester route; indeed, a contributing Act of that company for the S&H (Shrewsbury & Chester Act 1849) was passed.

Construction of the S&H line was contracted to Thomas Brassey, who also undertook to work it at his own cost and pay a dividend of $3\frac{1}{2}$%. Work commenced in 1850, with the first sod cut with great ceremony at Barrs Court, and Brassey opened the route from Shrewsbury to Ludlow as a single line on 21st April 1852. Work continued through to Hereford, opening for goods traffic on 30th July 1852 and for passengers on 6th December 1853. During the first few weeks, the line was worked by the Shrewsbury & Chester company's stock, until Brassey's own arrangements were completed.

Even as the construction of the S&H was in hand, there were plans afoot to make changes. The Great Western introduced a Traffic Arrangements Bill in 1851 in an attempt to convert the standard gauge into mixed gauge, a proposal that also involved the lines of the Shrewsbury & Birmingham, the Shrewsbury & Chester and others. This was not approved.

The S&H did not remain an isolated line for long, and in 1854 was connected with the NA&H at Hereford to provide a through route into South Wales. A number of other lines and branches were duly connected to the line, and these are shown in the summary Table *(page 170)*.

Such was the success of the line that by 1860, thanks to Brassey's endeavours, the S&H company were able to pay a dividend of 6%.

Of the railways that were to join the S&H route, the most significant was that of the Worcester & Hereford company, a standard gauge concern running via Malvern and Ledbury. This was the successful competitor in a number of proposals to join the two cities, one of which was another Brunel scheme, to be constructed to the mixed gauge. The W&H was to join with the S&H at Shelwick Jct., 1¾ miles north of the Barrs Court station, with a deviation from the S&H to Barton station authorised from Barrs Court Junction. The final section to Shelwick Jct. was completed in September 1861.

The West Midland company was formed in June 1860 (by the OW&W, W&H and NA&H companies), an amalgamation opposed by the S&H, but the outcome was that the latter secured running powers on from Hereford to Newport in exchange for the WMR gaining access to the Hereford & Shrewsbury line. The amalgamation of the WMR with the Great Western in 1863 sounded warning bells for the S&H, as they were now threatened by the GWR at both ends of their line, while the WMR soon opened their Worcester to Hereford and Severn Valley lines, which provided an alternative – if circuitous – route for traffic passing between Hereford and Shrewsbury.

Thomas Brassey's contract for the supply of locomotives and rolling stock for the line was by now coming to an end, and the S&H company were faced with having to provide these facilities for themselves. Confronted also with the threats to their security, the S&H directors therefore approached the London & North Western Railway, who had already opened a line from Crewe to Shrewsbury in 1858. Seizing the huge potential on offer to secure running powers through to South Wales, and especially to Merthyr – then the largest, most prosperous and industrially advanced location in Wales – the L&NWR directors made an offer of a perpetual lease of the S&H with a guaranteed 6% dividend on ordinary shares, but proposed that the GWR be invited to join with them as co-lessees. The GW saw through the L&NW's aspirations and, after a six month delay, rejected the offer.

The L&NW and S&H therefore promoted a joint bill in 1862 to enable the former to secure the lease on the line without Great Western participation, but reserved the right still to allow the GWR to join on terms to be agreed (Shrewsbury & Hereford Railway (Leasing) Act, 29th July 1862 S. 3). The Great Western and West Midland companies, somewhat knocked off course by the L&NW, opposed the bill fiercely, but were defeated and finally forced to join with the North Western in leasing the Shrewsbury & Hereford line. By that bill, effective on 1st July 1862, the line came under the control of the three concerns, though the WMR would of course soon amalgamate with the GWR.

Immediate arrangements were then made for doubling the line between Ludlow and Hereford, such work to the north of Ludlow having already been completed. The line through Dinmore Tunnel was, however, left single, and that section was not doubled until 1893.

All resources originally provided by Brassey were passed over to the new lessees, and management of the line entrusted to a Board of Directors composed of four members from both companies, with an independent chairman (to be appointed by the Board of Trade if not agreed mutually). Thus, the joint nature of the Shrewsbury & Hereford line was established.

TRAFFIC

THE EARLY YEARS

The first passenger trains to serve Shrewsbury ran on 16th October 1848 upon the opening of the Shrewsbury & Chester Railway. However, it was not until April 1852 that the S&H line was completed between Shrewsbury and Ludlow, with four passenger and one goods train in each direction providing the initial timetable. Beyond, a modest number of road connections were made with Hereford.

On 30th July 1852, the whole route was opened for goods traffic to Hereford, and for passengers on 6th December 1853. Again, four trains were operated over the line in each direction, with express, stopping, 'Parliamentary' and mixed (with goods) in evidence. The line was temporarily worked with Shrewsbury & Chester stock into a temporary station at Barrs Court, and then by Brassey's engines, with 2-2-2, 2-4-0 and 0-4-2 designs probably being utilised.

Shortly afterwards, a planned integration of S&H services at Hereford with the Newport, Abergavenny & Hereford company at their Barton station was proposed, but this was temporarily thwarted by the refusal of the Board of Trade to permit a junction to be built at Barrs Court to provide the necessary connection, and S&H trains continued to run into their Barrs Court station. For a short time, passengers had therefore to make their way across the city between the two stations in order to make connections, and few services were arranged to allow for this. The situation was resolved in January 1854 when the junction was installed to the north of Barrs Court station, and a connecting line to Barton was constructed: from this time, S&H traffic was diverted to use the temporary NA&H station, and services were arranged to connect.

This situation was interrupted in June 1855 when the Hereford, Ross & Gloucester company commenced their services into Barrs Court, and the Shrewsbury & Hereford left Barton to join them. The timetables of the S&H and HR&G were adjusted to provide connections, and disrupted the north-south flow. Once more, many through passengers were confronted with a cross-city journey between the stations, although a platform was soon provided at Barrs Court Junction to allow the interchange to take place there. This was followed by an arrangement whereby some NA&H trains ran through to Barrs Court.

At this time, the S&H route was uninterrupted between Shrewsbury and Hereford, though the first branch to connect with the line was opened in August 1857, between Leominster and Kington, with four services soon established in each direction, the two 'goods' services each way also conveying First and Second (and one 'Parliamentary') class passengers.

In 1861, a number of feeding/connecting routes were opened for traffic. The most important of these was the West Midland line from Worcester, which joined the S&H route at Shelwick Jct. for the last 1¾ miles into Hereford, giving direct connections from Paddington and Oxford, and from the industrial Midlands. One London express was soon running; departing from Paddington at 1.45 p.m., the Hereford portion was due into Barton station at 6.45 p.m., continuing through to Pontypool Road and Newport. The up service left Newport at 12.15 p.m., Hereford Barton at 1.50 p.m., and was due into Paddington at 6.35 p.m. Four other local passenger trains were established in each direction. Thus, Hereford's services were divided between its two main stations, although the reciprocal running arrangements saw a S&H service from Shrewsbury to Newport (and return), and a West Midland train over S&H metals on the same route. Pilot services continued to run between the two stations, and the interchange platform facilities at Barrs Court Jct.

A small number of goods trains were introduced over the Worcester line, with mineral/iron running between Dudley and Merthyr/Quaker's Yard, and goods to and from London. Local and pickup goods were also introduced.

Another arrival at this time was the 12¼-mile Knighton Railway, which opened from Craven Arms for goods traffic in 1860 and passenger trains in 1861. Four passenger services were provided between Craven Arms and Knighton in the early months of operations. The Knighton Railway was, however, a stepping stone to a much longer route, involving the Central Wales Railway from Knighton to Llandridnod Wells (19½ miles, opened in 1865) and the Central Wales Extension Railway from Llandridnod Wells to Llandovery (27½ miles, opened in 1868). From Llandovery, the Central Wales trains ran over the Vale of Towy line to Llandilo Jct., and over the Llanelly Railway & Dock metals to Pontardulais, where an independent line was provided via Killay to its terminus at Swansea Victoria (opened 1867). The section between Llandovery and Llandilo was leased, and came to operate as joint GWR and L&NWR, whilst running powers were exercised over the Llandilo to Pontardulais section. The three railways between the junctions at Craven Arms and Llandovery became part of the London & North Western empire in 1868, though that company had been involved with the route almost from the outset.

The Tenbury Railway commenced operations from Woofferton Junction in August 1861, with five trains in each direction soon forming the timetable. This branch was extended eastwards (by the Tenbury & Bewdley Railway) to join the Severn Valley line at Bewdley in 1864, with through running from Woofferton then taking place. The first section to Tenbury Jct. (just beyond the station) was GW and L&NW Joint, but Great Western property onwards to Bewdley (from 1869).

Just to the north, another joint line was opened in August 1861, the Ludlow & Clee Hill Railway. Unlike the others, this was essentially a mineral-only line, with services into Ludlow for disposal.

From July 1862, the S&H line was leased jointly to the L&NW, the Great Western & West Midland, who shared the locomotives between them; the GW/WM allotment included six 2-2-2s, a 2-4-0, four 0-4-2s and four 0-6-0s.

The next company to appear over S&H metals was the Bishop's Castle Railway, which had negotiated running powers with the S&H Joint Committee in October 1865 to operate the three-quarters-of-a-mile from Stretford Jct. into Craven Arms station, where the facilities were used. The services were modest, with four return journeys initially, decreasing to just two over the years.

A further change to the railway scene at Hereford occurred in August 1866 with the completion of the L&NW's Hereford Curve, running from the Gloucester line at Rotherwas Jct. to Red Hill Jct. on the NA&H route, permitting through services to operate through Barrs Court to and from Newport. Most services from that point then ran via Barrs Court, leaving primarily the Midland Railway's services from Brecon at Barton station, though with Midland or Great Western coaches being taken by the Pilots to and from either Barrs Court Jct. or Barrs Court stations, in connection with main line trains on the Worcester route.

On 16th December 1867, the third branch line utilising Craven Arms station was opened for traffic when the Wenlock Railway reached Marsh Farm Jct., a little more than three miles to the north of Craven Arms, from Presthope. This was the last link of a through route from Wellington (via Lightmoor Jct, Buildwas and Much Wenlock) involving three other small railways, which had been otherwise completed in 1864. Through services between Craven Arms and Wellington commenced, the timetable soon settling at three or four each way.

As the century progressed, the Great Western acquired the Much Wenlock (1896), New Radnor etc., (1897/8) and Bromyard (1888) branches, whilst the Joint Committee absorbed the Clee Hill (1893) and Tenbury (1869) lines. The former group had, to various degrees, been worked by the GWR in earlier years, as had the latter by the S&H or Joint bodies. The Bishop's Castle (independent) and Central Wales (L&NW) lines remained in their former ownerships. Little change was therefore experienced in stock or timetables.

VICTORIAN DEVELOPMENTS

In 1876, there were two down expresses, each calling only at Ludlow and Leominster, though none in the up direction. However, there were three semi-fast up trains calling additionally at Woofferton, Craven Arms and Church Stretton, with one in the down direction. These connected at Hereford with Worcester & South Wales, and/or Hereford & Gloucester services, and variously conveyed through coaches between Birkenhead or Shrewsbury and Hereford, Gloucester, Cheltenham, Swindon, Cardiff or Swansea. A through First/Second Luggage Compo coach between Kington and Paddington was also conveyed each way. These services usually comprised between four and seven 6-wheel coaches.

There were three local passenger services in each direction, calling at all fifteen intermediate stations, usually taking around 2½ hours for the journey.

In addition, there was one return 'short' local train between Ludlow and Shrewsbury, and between Leominster and Hereford daily to supplement the local trains.

The Woofferton and Bewdley branch passenger service was at this time operated from Ludlow and Leominster, with a coaching set from each utilised for the timetable. During the day, these provided one connection each way between Leominster and Woofferton, and two between Ludlow and Woofferton (three on Mondays).

Also on the scene was an overnight through fast goods service in each direction between Bristol, Birkenhead and Manchester, running via Gloucester and Hereford; this would develop into one of the Great Western's express vacuum trains in later years, though routed via the Severn Tunnel.

Through Great Western goods trains also operated over the S&H line, running mainly between Llanelly or Pontypool Road and Birkenhead or Manchester.

By far the greatest number of GWR goods movements over the S&H line was made by the Pontypool Road and Birkenhead coal trains, with balancing empties southbound. A few of these ran through from or to Nantyglo or Ebbw Vale, but the majority were marshalled at Pontypool Road. Most were conditional – running 'when required' – but the number of paths allocated to them totalled around fifteen per day at this time.

Also running over the joint line were two or three local goods trains each way between Shrewsbury and Hereford. On the southern portion of the line, a local service ran from Hartlebury and Woofferton to Leominster and back, calling at Berrington when required.

Another set of semi-fast passenger trains over the joint line at this time were L&NW services to Pontypool Road and Newport (Mill Street), three services running each way daily. These did not survive for long, and had gone by 1882.

As well as sharing in the joint passenger services between Shrewsbury and Hereford, the L&NW continued to run one or two through Central Wales trains between Shrewsbury, Craven Arms and Swansea in each direction. Most of the six passenger services traversing the Central Wales line each way started or terminated at Craven Arms, connecting with S&H trains to and from Shrewsbury.

L&NW Goods services originating from both the Stafford (via Wellington) and Crewe lines at Shrewsbury frequently ran through to Abergavenny Jct. along the S&H Joint, or to Swansea via Craven Arms and the Central Wales line. These are mostly recorded as working to and from London, Birmingham, Burton, Liverpool and Manchester. Others originated or terminated at Coleham.

Like the Great Western, the L&NW operated many through coal and empties trains from and to South Wales, though in this instance mostly between Birkenhead and Abergavenny Jct. In addition, there were a number of Loco Coal trains to (and empties from) Rugby, Stafford, Crewe, Coleham and Chester. In all, there were up to seventeen L&NW coal movements each way daily, depending upon which of the conditional services ran.

The primary Great Western engines on faster services were 2-2-2s, including the '69' and 'Sir Daniel' classes, and some of the earlier 2-4-0s, such as the 'Chancellor' design.

The final branch to connect with the S&H route was the Leominster & Bromyard Railway, opened to Steens Bridge on 1st March 1884, and on to Bromyard in September 1897. This completed another through route, this time from Worcester (The Worcester, Bromyard & Leominster Railway), which had reached Bromyard in 1877. As was seemingly traditional, four return journeys were introduced over the line to Steens Bridge.

On 1st December 1886, the Severn Tunnel opened for passenger traffic. Some nineteen months later, on 1st July 1888, a service of three express passenger trains in each direction between Crewe and Bristol was inaugurated, conveying through coaches between the North of England and Bristol in connection with the Great Western's West Country services. All stopped at Shrewsbury, where engine changes were also carried out, and at Hereford. The through carriages scheduled in July 1890 on the four trains then running each way gave connections between Bristol, Manchester and Liverpool on each service; on three trains for Birkenhead; on two for Glasgow; and on one for Leeds. Vehicles also ran from Taunton to Manchester, Liverpool and Birkenhead on one train. Through coaches to and from Cardiff were also conveyed, serving Manchester, Liverpool and Newcastle on one train each way, and Birkenhead on two. 'Chancellor' class 2-4-0s were primarily in charge of these services at the outset.

The installation of standard gauge track beyond Exeter in May 1892 brought Devon and Cornwall into the scope of the through coaches. The introduction of these was quite modest at the outset: in the summer of 1893, through coaches between Kingswear and Manchester, Liverpool, Birkenhead and Leeds were in operation on one train, Plymouth and Glasgow on another, and overnight between Penzance and Manchester. Not all ran in both directions. The Bristol coaches still ran as previously on the four trains. Thus, the fundamental arrangement of the North & West services was established.

Locomotives working the North & West Bristol express passenger services between Shrewsbury and Hereford in the 1890s were mostly the new '3232' class 2-4-0s, with '111', '439', 'Stella', and ex-West Midland classes recorded on other fast and local services. Various 0-6-0s and 0-4-2Ts were used on the local passenger services, whilst goods trains were hauled by 0-6-0s, including tanks, even for longer-distance duties such as the Pontypool & Birkenhead coal.

The first corridor stock was introduced onto the Great Western in 1892, but no such luxury was provided for the North & West route in the last decade of the nineteenth century. By the summer of 1899, the through services had expanded to seven or eight in each direction daily, and in the summer period, the West Country and South Wales services warranted separate trains, though the reduction to six for the winter timetable brought about some combining of stock, usually divided (or joined) at Hereford. All the main stock was 8-wheel, with toilet accommodation in most.

THE NEW CENTURY

From the turn of the century, Great Western locomotives in use on the through Shrewsbury & Hereford services were mostly of the 4-4-0 classes, with almost all designs appearing in the period up to the Great War: 'Bulldog', 'Duke', 'County', 'Badminton', 'City' and 'Atbara' classes were recorded on express and fast services. Engines on local trains were varied, and included some 4-4-0s, '56' and '2201' 2-4-0s, 'Standard', '57 and '2301' class 0-6-0s, with '517' 'Metros and '1076' tanks on shorter-distance services. Goods were still largely of the 0-6-0 designs, although '26XX' class 2-6-0s were increasingly to be seen.

L&NW engines on the line by this time included 2-2-2s of the 'Lady of the Lake' class, along with 2-4-0s and 0-6-0s of various designs. Some of the compound 2-2-2-2s and 2-2-2-0s were also utilised in the area.

A variety of classes were to be seen at the junctions on the connecting branch services, including Steam Railmotors and '517s' at Craven Arms on the Wellington route; '517s' and '1501s' at Woofferton on Tenbury & Bewdley trains; '655' and '2021' classes on the Leominster and New Radnor (etc.) services; and '517s' and 'Standard Goods' on the Leominster, Bromyard and Worcester trains.

Corridor trains started to appear on North & West trains in the autumn of 1904. The first regular set ran as the 12.6 p.m. from Weston-super-Mare, comprising a Great Western Brake Tri-Compo (from Kingswear to Liverpool), L&NW Dining Car (Bristol to Liverpool), GWR Brake Third (Weston to Liverpool) and L&NW Tri-Compo (Weston to Manchester). The set returned at 10.30 a.m. Liverpool and 10.45 a.m. Manchester (11.40 a.m. Crewe). By summer 1906, this had grown to an eight-coach L&NW corridor train from Bristol (now 9.30 a.m.), with a vehicle for Leeds included. There was also a three-coach corridor section of Caledonian and West Coast Joint stock for Edinburgh, Glasgow and Aberdeen on an earlier train from Bristol.

With the evolution of the North & West express services, the last summer of peace in 1914 witnessed seven daily North & West services in each direction, now for the most part formed of corridor stock, largely Great Western and North Western. There were also two dining car trains in each direction, with L&NW cars working between Liverpool and Bristol, and GWR vehicles between Plymouth and Liverpool. The through coaches ran mostly between Penzance, Plymouth, Kingswear or Bristol and Manchester or Liverpool, though with one or two to Birkenhead, Glasgow or Edinburgh. South Wales portions connected Cardiff with Birkenhead, Manchester, Liverpool or Newcastle. The Birkenhead coaches of these trains were added or detached at Shrewsbury, some conveyed by London trains.

The L&NW began to use 4-4-0s and 'Experiment' 4-6-0s on their North & West duties in this period.

Passenger stock of local trains on the S&H was also provided by both companies, often with five, six or seven-coach trains of 6-wheel stock. There were now nine local services between Shrewsbury and Hereford, together with a few intermediate services variously between Shrewsbury, Craven Arms, Ludlow and Hereford, which were mostly worked by the Shrewsbury & Hereford coaches.

Even the L&NW's Central Wales line now saw a comprehensive arrangement of through coaches, with vehicles for Swansea from Euston, Birmingham, Manchester, Liverpool, Llandudno and Blackpool scheduled in the summer months, via Shrewsbury. In total, there were around eight passenger trains each way at Craven Arms (a couple of which worked through from or to Shrewsbury) increasingly hauled by Bowen-Cooke's new 4-6-2Ts.

Whilst passenger services had seen vast improvements over the years, freight operations had also been developed. The main advancement here was the introduction of fast, vacuum-fitted overnight goods trains, hauled frequently by passenger engines. Those running over the N&W route included the Bristol & Birkenhead and Cardiff & Birkenhead.

In terms of ordinary Great Western freights, the N&W line had decreased to around ten. It is very likely that this was a minimal figure, and that Control added more to the total, particularly coal and empties on a 'run as required' basis.

L&NW freights continued to work through from the Crewe and Stafford lines, destined mainly for Abergavenny or Swansea.

Traffic over the various branch lines connecting to the North & West line had approached a zenith. Woofferton saw ten passenger

A southbound North & West service near Bayston Hill box, on the outskirts of Shrewsbury, double-headed by Coleham '43XX' class 2–6–0 No. 4352 and a 'Saint' 4–6–0, c.1924. The train was composed of around 14 bogies, possibly with a van on the rear, and typical of the heavy loading of these services at busy summer periods.
REAL PHOTOGRAPHS

Standing at the south end of No. 5 platform at Shrewsbury station, former 4–4–2 'Scott' No. 2990 *Waverley* awaiting departure with what was probably a North & West express in the early/mid 1930s. This engine was a familiar sight at Shrewsbury in the interwar period, being stationed at Stafford Road, Coleham and Chester between 1920 and 1932, and Canton from 1932 until withdrawal from service in late 1938. With the branding 'CDF' just visible on her right-hand lamp, it is likely that she was bound for South Wales with the express, the first vehicle of which was a clerestory coach. These were still quite common on fast services at the time.
PHOTOMATIC

Hereford ex-L&NW shed, looking north c.1936. The shed was located between Barrs Court Junction and Barrs Court station, on the eastern side of the running lines at the northern end of the LMS's goods facilities. Brecon Curve, with the signal box of that name, can be seen just beyond, diverging to the left of the four running lines.   STEPHENSON LOCOMOTIVE SOCIETY COLLECTION

and three goods movements in each direction, whilst the Much Wenlock & Wellington line at Craven Arms provided three passenger and one goods daily each way. The Bishop's Castle line also worked four trains into and out of Craven Arms. There were four or five mineral or empties movements on the Clee Hill line at Ludlow.

At Leominster, eight passenger, mixed and goods movements in each direction worked over the Kington & New Radnor branch, with five passenger and one goods each way on the Bromyard & Worcester line.

German submarine activity in the 1914 war caused a large reduction in coastal shipping, with resultant problems for the N&W line in having to cope with the flow of Admiralty 'Jellicoe Specials' from Pontypool to Scapa Flow, supplying steam coal to the British fleet. The previous manner of supplying the fleet by coastal colliers was now considered to be too dangerous. These trains ran with priority over most others. Such were the problems of line occupancy that some 'Jellicoes' had to be diverted to alternative routes on the Great Western, and even over the Cambrian between Brecon and Oswestry. In all, some 13,000 Admiralty specials were run over the duration of the conflict, with '28XX' class 2-8-0s taking the brunt of the traffic on the Great Western.

Whilst locomotive usage on express passenger duties over the route in recent times had been very largely four-coupled designs, the age of the Great Western 4-6-0 effectively appeared in the summer of 1914 with the use of 'Saints' on the North & West services, although the 4-4-0 'Counties' were also still much used on these trains.

Passenger services mostly retained their pre-war levels at the outset, but from 1917 the drain on manpower and materials caused a reduction. The eight peacetime N&W express services were reduced

to five, trains were heavier, schedules slower, and dining carriages severely reduced.

FROM THE GROUPING

It was not until 1922 that the timetable bore much resemblance to the prewar version. Seven fast trains were now running daily over the N&W route, three with dining cars. The basis for express services in the 'twenties and 'thirties had been established.

In the very early years, parcels, mail, stores and other similar traffic by passenger train could be either carried by vehicles within or attached to regular services, but as the system expanded and the traffic increased, dedicated parcels trains were required to cope with the amounts being moved daily. By the early 1920s, the North & West route saw the 3.25 and 11.55 a.m. Crewe to Bristol, and the 1.0 p.m. Penzance to Crewe.

As the 1920s progressed, the 'Saints' became ever more present on the express services over the N&W line, followed at the end of the decade by 'Star' class locomotives, mostly displaced from West of England services by 'Castles' and 'Kings'.

The 'Halls' appeared in 1929, and a few were soon to be seen on goods turns, particularly on the vacuum services. They also gradually worked into the passenger rosters as their numbers increased.

Another new class to enter traffic, in 1936, were the 'Granges', and these were soon at work in the area on goods trains.

In the 1930s, the N&W line saw Stanier designs introduced in modest numbers, with 2-6-0s, '8F' 2-8-0s and Class '5' 4-6-0s appearing.

The express passenger trains in winter 1930/1 amounted to six in each direction, now hauled predominantly by 'Star' class engines. There were eight local passenger services over the length of the line, with a couple more running as far south as Ludlow. In addition, the Tenbury line trains visited both Leominster and Ludlow as part of their schedules.

There were four through Central Wales passenger trains running through to or from Shrewsbury, with four or five others originating or terminating at Craven Arms.

Very considerable freight traffic was evident over the line, particularly in the northern section. The important GWR vacuum services led the way, with three each way between Birkenhead or Manchester and Cardiff or Bristol. Great Western daily through traffic ran mostly from Saltney or Shrewsbury and Hereford or Pontypool Road, with a few into South Wales. There were also a number of local turns between Shrewsbury. Ludlow and/or Hereford.

LMS freights were divided mainly between Swansea (via Llandovery) and Abergavenny (via Hereford), with up to ten over the Central Wales route and a similar number over the Joint line. Many of these had 0-8-0s, although a number of faster trains had mixed traffic types. As well as Shrewsbury, these trains originated/terminated at Crewe, Edge Hill, Heaton Norris, Copley Hill, Stafford, Burton, Bescot and Rugby. Fish and perishables also ran in season.

The first closure of a railway utilising the N&W route occurred in the mid-'thirties with the withdrawal of services over the Bishop's Castle line in April 1935. It was not until 1937 that the junction and signals were removed.

Unlike at the outbreak of the First World War, the start of hostilities in 1939 prompted an immediate reduction in passenger services to allow emergency arrangements – evacuation, troop movements and other urgent matters – to be effected. Only three of the North & West through passenger services were retained in each direction.

Matters were gradually improved as the war continued, and by 1943 six express and seven local services were running in each direction, though the timings of the faster trains bore little resemblance to their peacetime equivalents. The movement of troops and stores was extremely heavy at times, whilst 'Government Stores' trains conveying all the necessities of war were a common sight, though few people were aware of their contents.

The cessation of hostilities in 1945 did not bring about an immediate return to normality, and it was some three or four years before matters improved significantly. A considerable backlog of work, and shortages of men and materials prolonged the wartime atmosphere into the period of austerity, beyond the 1948 Nationalization.

By the summer of 1949, all had virtually returned to normal in terms of express services, with a transformation of North & West services; the usual eight services were once again running on weekdays, but there were now thirteen on Saturdays, primarily to and from the Manchester and Liverpool areas, though with Glasgow, Preston and Blackpool also featuring. In addition, there were seven or eight late or overnight trains southbound to the West Country to ease the Saturday congestion, but the return from the West Country was largely carried out on Saturdays.

After the wartime peak, goods services were now returning to a peacetime level of around fifteen over the N&W route, and the usual dozen or so LMR services from the Crewe and Stafford lines to Swansea and Abergavenny, each way

THE NORTH & WEST IN THE 1950s.

The North & West route had become the most important cross-country line on the GWR/Western Region, with the majority of services linking Manchester and Liverpool with South Wales, Bristol, and the West of England daily, though also with through coach working to and from Glasgow and Birkenhead. During the summer months, traffic increased substantially, with services to and from Somerset, Devon and Cornwall.

As working class communities became more affluent during the 1950s, and were able to take holidays in the West Country, many more services by night as well as by day ran over the North & West line, with main trains also divided into two and more parts, and those trains that usually amalgamated at Crewe from Liverpool and Manchester now running through as independent trains. Summer Saturdays saw trains from Manchester starting at London Road, Victoria, Mayfield and Central stations bound for Paignton, Kingswear and Penzance, as well as through trains from Glasgow, all with balancing return workings. Other Saturday destinations in the North included Blackpool and Preston, with through portions from Birkenhead.

Almost all trains changed engines at Shrewsbury in the 1950s, with mostly Western Region locomotives working the N&W. The exception was on the through trains which used to run to and from the ex-L&NWR line from Merthyr and Tredegar, both booked services and excursions, which changed engines at Abergavenn Junction, using LMS 4-6-0s working through from and to Crewe. There was, however, one long-term Longsight (Manchester) turn through to Pontypool Road from 1950 until 1962, perpetuating the joint nature of the line, and well recorded by photographers along the entire length of the line.

Clearance for 'Kings' through the Severn Tunnel saw three of the engines allocated to Bath Road, Bristol, from 1948 to 1950/2, including No.6000 King George V itself, which worked regularly to Shrewsbury on the 4.30 p.m. from Bristol, whilst later, Cardiff 'Kings' worked the three main Canton turns to Shrewsbury between 1960 and 1962. Canton 'Britannias' had featured on these turns since 1952, increasingly so when all the WR fleet of these engines were allocated to Cardiff between 1957 and 1961. A feature of the line was the working of a Shrewsbury and Newton Abbot top link 'Castle' through on alternate days on a lodging turn, which again features significantly in the photographs reproduced here.

The line witnessed a number of closures in the early 1950s. The Wellington and Much Wenlock passenger services were withdrawn in 1951, with one freight and three passenger movements into and out of Craven Arms at the end.

From Leominster, the branch lines served via Kington also experienced some downgrading, with the Radnor and Presteign sections closed to passenger services from 1951; five passenger and one freight trains were in operation to either Kington or New Radnor in those final months. A service of four passenger (five on Saturdays) was maintained to Kington, with one freight to Dolyhir and Presteign. Passenger services were finally withdrawn in February 1955, though the freight trains continued into the mid-1960s.

The Bromyard branch from Leominster was another early casualty, in September 1952. The late movements on the branch were five Down and six Up passenger services, with three Down and two Up freight movements.

In the mid-1950s, the North & West saw a regular service of through general goods trains between Cardiff or Pontypool Road and Coton Hill, Wrexham or Saltney Yard (from where traffic was re-marshalled for ongoing destinations in Manchester, Liverpool, the North, and Scotland). About twenty services operated in each direction, plus a couple of local trips between Shrewsbury and Hereford. Around ten through goods trains each way ran over the Central Wales line to and from the Swansea area, including a few extended beyond Shrewsbury to and from Crewe, Burton and Stafford, maintaining a little of the original L&NW flow.

The WR through goods services were hauled by '28XXs', 'WDs', '30XXs', 'Granges', 'Halls' and '43XXs', with '2251' 0-6-0s on the more local trains. Even the last of the Dean '2301' class was to be occasionally seen at Shrewsbury, working its last days out at Oswestry until withdrawal in 1957. On the LMR side, 'Class 5s', Stanier

2-8-0s and some of the old ex-L&NW 'G2' 0-8-0s were to be seen, as well as BR Standard designs.

In June 1958, the North & West route between Shrewsbury and Hereford was dealt a blow with the closure of the smaller intermediate passenger stations, leaving only Church Stretton, Craven Arms, Ludlow, Woofferton and Leominster in operation. Goods services lingered on for a while in some cases.

The Woofferton and Tenbury Wells branch was closed to passenger and goods traffic in July 1961, though the section from Tenbury to Bewdley continued for another year with passenger trains, and a little longer for freight. Woofferton station was closed at this time.

Mineral traffic over the Clee Hill branch survived until 1962, and its closure left just the Central Wales and Worcester lines in con-

nection with the northern half of the N&W route to see out the final years of steam.

Electrification of the West Coast Main Line out of Euston, during the 1960s, had a very significant effect on the Shrewsbury and Hereford line. North & West services to and from the West Country were diverted to run via Birmingham (New Street), whilst semi-fast and local trains running through to Hereford or South Wales served the intermediate stations at Church Stretton, Craven Arms, Ludlow and Leominster.

Traditional freight services gradually dwindled, leaving just block trains or Freightliner container traffic running with the passenger services.

A glimpse of a bygone era with 'City' class 4-4-0 No.3440 *City of Truro* accelerating out of Sutton Bridge Jct. towards Bayston Hill box on Tuesday, 27th May 1958, with the return Shrewsbury to Cardiff Special, hauling a respectable load of nine coaches. This engine was taken out of York Museum early in 1957 and restored to running condition, primarily to work specials, although she was used on ordinary trains when not so engaged. No.3440 was allocated to Didcot around this time, and finally returned to York in 1961. The junction with the Severn Valley line was just beyond the road overbridge in the distance, and that to Welshpool near the rear coaches of the train, diverging to the left. Shelf Sidings feature to the right of the running lines.
RUSSELL MULFORD

'Hall' No.5986 *Arbury Hall* with what was probably the 2.32 p.m. Crewe to Pontypool Road parcels picking up speed as it headed for Bayston Hill in 1955. No.5986 had been transferred from Old Oak to Shrewsbury (Coleham) shed in October 1954, and was in Stafford Road Works for five days in February/March 1955 for attention, to which its repainted smokebox was probably testament. Regular traffic on this service was from Scotland and Northern England to Cardiff, with a small number of vehicles for Bristol and the South West, connecting at Pontypool Road. It ran on Saturdays, but only as required on other days. Beyond the train, the curve of the S & M line on its embankment as it turned around to the north (and Abbey station) is clearly visible in this view.
RUSSELL MULFORD

A frustrating run was probably ahead for the returning Newton Abbot crew of 'Castle' No.4098 *Kidwelly Castle*, which was leaking steam badly and obscuring the road ahead. The train was the 9.10 a.m. Liverpool to Plymouth, heading towards Bayston Hill in late June 1954, and passing the Sutton Bridge advance starter, which also carried the Bayston Hill distant, still on. The first four coaches were destined for Paignton (Kingswear on Saturdays), with the remainder (six scheduled) for Plymouth, including a dining car. Four further vehicles were carried on Saturdays on this busy train. The steel bridge over the rear of the train carried the Abbey station (Shrewsbury & Montgomery) line over the Hereford route.
RUSSELL MULFORD

TOWARDS BAYSTON HILL

As we have seen in Volume One, the junctions at Sutton Bridge saw the divergence of the Severn Valley route to the left at the south end of the Coleham complex, and of the Welshpool and Minsterley lines to the right a little further to the south (0m 67ch). From that point, Shelf Sidings accompanied the Shrewsbury & Hereford route on its eastern side until that line was spanned by the Shropshire & Montgomeryshire Light railway. There were just a pair of sidings in 1900, though with no Relief lines until around 1914. Two more sidings were added to Shelf, probably around the First World War. Beyond the S & MLR bridge, the main line was flanked by Up and Down Relief lines only.

The four-track section continued southwards only for a short distance beyond the S & M bridge before the Down Relief joined its Main line, leaving a three-track section to continue onwards to Bayston Hill signal box, some three-quarters of a mile to the south of the bridge. At Bayston Hill box (1m 65ch), the Up Relief also joined with the Main, leaving two tracks to continue on a lengthy straight section towards the Bayston Hill curves.

The four-track section from Sutton Bridge Jct. ran to a point underneath the S & M overbridge at Bayston Hill, where the down goods loop was connected to the main, though a spur ran on for a short distance, seen here to the right. Landore 'Hall' No.6903 *Belmont Hall* is seen getting away past clear signals with a southbound express in late June 1954, probably bound for South Wales.

RUSSELL MULFORD

Shrewsbury's Standard 'Class 5' No.73034 heading a southbound freight on the approach to Bayston Hill in late June 1954. This was one of the five engines of the class at Coleham 'on loan' from the Scottish Region, working, alongside eight similarly acquired from the London Midland. As with the 'Halls', they were mainly used for passenger and fast freight duties, the latter mainly in the Crewe and Stafford (LMR) routes, though also to Cardiff and Swansea (Victoria) to the south of Shrewsbury.

RUSSELL MULFORD

Modified 'Hall' No.6976 *Grayhwaite Hall* heading the 8.5 p.m. Dorrington to Marylebone Milk away from the Bayston Hill area near Shelf Sidings in 1954. This was an unusual service, commenced about 1936 to convey milk from the Independent Milk Supplies' premises at Dorrington to their Rossmore Road dairy on the approach to Marylebone station, on the former Great Central line. The Great Western conveyed the milk to Banbury, where it was handed over to the L & NE, who took it via Woodford to Marylebone. In BR days, the milk was worked more logically from Banbury, along the 'new' line via Bicester to the GW&GC, thence to Marylebone. No.6976 was a Banbury engine, working the milk to her home station from where an ER locomotive took it on.

RUSSELL MULFORD

Pwllheli '2251' Class 0-6-0 No.2232 heading south on the approach to Bayston Hill with the class 'C' empty milk tanks from Marylebone to Dorrington in 1958. Doubtless, the engine had been commandeered for the task before working back to the Coast section, though Pwllheli/Porthmadoc '2251' engines did not usually run further east than Welshpool by this time. The milk traffic to Marylebone traditionally ran under 'C' lamps, as did the empties back to Shrewsbury, and the transfer to Coleham. They were in one period scheduled to be attached at Shelf Sidings to the 8.10 a.m. Shrewsbury to Craven Arms local freight ('K'), and later taken by the 7.30 a.m. Abbey Foregate to Dorrington.

RUSSELL MULFORD

The Summer Saturday 12.30 p.m. Paignton to Manchester service, loaded to nine bogies for London Road station, leaving the Bayston Hill area behind Bath Road 'Castle' No.5067 *St. Fagans Castle*, c. 1953. Shortly afterwards, the train identification number '593' was transferred to the 5.15 p.m. Paignton to Nottingham service, and the 'noon' train from Paignton to Manchester adopted '594'. RUSSELL MULFORD

A northbound class 'C' parcels train nearing Shelf Sidings in 1958 behind Old Oak 'Hall' No.4977 *Watcombe Hall*, with the Meole Brace (A5) overbridge in the distance. This may have been the 8.5 p.m. Dorrington milk, as there appears to be two or three tanks and a passenger brake van behind the tender. The end of the up relief line's spur can be seen to the left, with the stop block against the Rea Brook cutting. RUSSELL MULFORD

Shrewsbury's Class '5' No.45143 makes a fine sight on the approach to the A5 road overbridge near Bayston Hill signal box with the 12.5 p.m. Central Wales service from Shrewsbury to Swansea Victoria, having just passed that box's home signal. The train was formed of four corridor coaches in the carmine and cream livery of the early 1950s, with the 'classic' Van Third, Compo, Third, Van Third arrangement, with what was probably the Shrewsbury to Llandovery van on the rear.

Having passed beneath the A5 road bridge, and with Bayston Hill box ahead, No.45143 was heading the same Central Wales service, with a badly-leaking steam pipe between the second and third coaches. The coach set was scheduled for a two-day cycle, balancing with the 12.25 p.m. Swansea to Shrewsbury, alternating with a similar set on these two trains. Many of the Central Wales services working to or from Shrewsbury consisted of five coaches, with an additional Th:d included.
RUSSELL MULFORD

No. 45143 is seen here again with the four-coach 12.5 p.m. (12.30 p.m. Saturdays) service to Swansea Victoria, this time without the Llandovery van, as it approached, the A5 overbridge in 1955. This was a lightweight load for the '5MT', which was probably working the three-day, three engine Coleham turn which took it to Swansea on the first day, back the following day with the 12.25 p.m. Swansea before working on to Crewe, and a Crewe to Swansea (9.50 p.m. York) and Shrewsbury duty on the third. RUSSELL MULFORD

A very grimy Stanier '8F' No.48761 with a northbound freight easing along the up goods loop just to the south of the A5 overbridge on 24th September 1960. This engine was stationed at Llanelly, having been transferred there from Swansea Paxton Street in September 1959, when that shed closed. It was almost certainly on a Central Wales freight. The houses of Meole Brace can be seen in the background.
MICHAEL MENSING

Passing the Bayston Hill home signal, Longsight 'Jubilee' No.45638 *Zanzibar* was in the charge of Shrewsbury men as it headed the 9.25 a.m. Manchester (London Road) to Cardiff and Swansea service in 1953. She worked through to Pontypool Road and would return with the 7.40 a.m. Penzance train later in the day. This service conveyed coaches from Manchester to Swansea at the head, then a section for Cardiff, with either a pair of coaches from Crewe to Cardiff (Saturdays only) or Birkenhead to Cardiff (Saturdays excepted). RUSSELL MULFORD

Approaching the A5 bridge near Bayston Hill box, Shrewsbury 'Castle' No.5073 *Blenheim* is pictured during late 1955 after returning from a heavy repair at Swindon. She was working the double-home turn (Salop 50) to Newton Abbot – the 9.5 a.m. Liverpool to Plymouth – returning the following day with the 8.0 a.m. Plymouth. No.5073 was one of two 'Castles' with a long history at Shrewsbury; *Blenheim* was there from February 1939 (as *Cranbrook Castle* until January 1941) to March 1958, when she was moved to Bath Road as part of the mileage equalization exercise.
RUSSELL MULFORD

Viewed late one morning in 1952, a north-bound goods service had just joined the up loop at Bayston Hill box, with an ex-L & NW '7F' 0-8-0, still carrying 'LMS' on the tender, at the head. At this time, Shrewsbury, Swansea and Abergavenny all housed these engines, and they were therefore a very common sight on this section of the line. The goods train was quite mixed, and seems to have been conveying mineral, general merchandise, industrial and oil traffic.   RUSSELL MULFORD

The same train had just passed beneath the A5 overbridge, and was heading away towards Sutton Bridge Jct. on the approach to Shrewsbury. The former private owner wagon, third on the train, still showed its former ownership – Carlton – on the side; this company operated mines in South Yorkshire, including the famous Grimethorpe pit.

RUSSELL MULFORD

To the south of Bayston Hill box – which can be seen beyond the coaches of the train on the down (right) side of the line – the S & H route became two-track, and was soon forced to divert south-eastwards around higher ground on which stood Bayston Hill village. Here, the final 'Grange', Oxley's No.6879 *Overton Grange*, was clearing Bayston Hill box and heading for Condover with a train formed of carmine & cream stock, c.1953.

RUSSELL MULFORD

The tight bend at Bayston Hill is well illustrated in this view of the same service as the 'Grange' was easing her train around the first curve near the occupation bridge. The maximum speed on the line was shown as 75 mph, but was reduced to 60 for the half-mile around the Bayston curves.

RUSSELL MULFORD

BAYSTON HILL

About a quarter-mile beyond Bayston Hill box, the line curved to the left (south-east) to avoid the hill upon which stood the village of Bayston Hill, then curved to the right (south-west) to pick up its original alignment out of Shrewsbury again. Half-way round the divergence, it passed between Bayston and Sharpstone Hills, the latter being the site of quarrying to this day.

Viewed from the occupation bridge, Shrewsbury 'County' No.1003 *County of Wilts* is seen rounding the curve on her way towards Bayston Hill box with the 8.45 a.m. Plymouth to Liverpool (front) and Manchester service, with a dining car in the Manchester portion. The 8.45 a.m. Plymouth was scheduled for stock of both the Western and London Midland regions, mixed in this case between the two sections. A rather unusual – and substantial – structure with an attached platform section can be seen on the embankment to the right of the engine, with the ground cut away between it and the trackwork; this may have been concerned with permanent way work, given its remote location.   RUSSELL MULFORD

Sweeping round the tight bend at Bayston Hill, a 'Hall' was heading north on Summer Saturday service 579, the 9.5 a.m. Paignton to Manchester (London Road), which was due into Shrewsbury at 3.7 p.m. In this period, it was usual for a Newton Abbot 'Hall' to take the train to Pontypool Road, and a Chester 'Hall' to bring it into Shrewsbury. As was the case with many of the Saturdays-only North & West holiday services, the entire train ran through from origin to destination, with no through vehicles for or from other points.

RUSSELL MULFORD

Heading towards Bayston Hill box, Standard Class '4' No.75006 passing under the occupation bridge on the Bayhill curve c.1953 with an up local. Ten new '75XXXs' were allocated to Coleham shed in autumn 1951, but were all transferred away to Swindon and Cardiff in September/October 1953; No.75006 went to Cardiff initially, but was soon moved to Oswestry, for Cambrian services, from where she would doubtless have made an occasional visit to Shrewsbury once more.
RUSSELL MULFORD

The tight bends just to the north-east of Bayston Hill village feature in these views of Standard Class '4' No.75053 returning to Shrewsbury with wagons of spent ballast on Sunday, 9th May 1965. The first view shows the engine with five Engineer's wagons sandwiched between two brake vans, whilst in the distance is the bridge carrying the Sharpstone Hill lane over the railway. The second photograph, taken moments later, shows the train approaching the occupation bridge over the curve leading towards Bayston Hill signal box.
MICHAEL MENSING

Passing over relaid track under the Sharpstone Hill bridge, Bayston Hill, on 24th September 1960, Shrewsbury-based Stanier '8F' 2-8-0 No.48735 was working the 10.25 a.m. Swansea Victoria to Shrewsbury. Though passenger services on this line were normally worked by Class '5' 4-6-0s. 2-6-4Ts and sometimes by a 'Jubilee', '8Fs' were not unknown as a means of rebalancing power at the Swansea end; many worked there on freight duties over the line from Shrewsbury.
MICHAEL MENSING

A freight for Swansea climbing around Bayston Hill curves on Saturday, 24th September 1960 behind Llanelly Stanier '8F' No.48419. The engine had just passed beneath the Sharpstone Hill bridge, on the easier grades towards Condover. The vehicles visible on the train were still recognizable company or early BR designs, including the ex-GWR 5-plank, 13-ton former 'Open B' No.W136054, second behind the tender, built in the latter 1930s.
MICHAEL MENSING

The double-home Shrewsbury turn to Newton Abbot, worked by No.7025 *Sudeley Castle*, is seen easing over a permanent way slack through Bayston Hill curves on 24th September 1960. This was the 8.0 a.m. Plymouth to Liverpool and Kingswear to Manchester, with through coaches from Plymouth to Glasgow ('M87'). No.7025 went to Shrewsbury in August 1960 after 11 years at Old Oak Common, and in 1962 was transferred to Worcester. New in August 1949, she had run almost 686,000 miles when withdrawn.

MICHAEL MENSING

A woebegone Pontypool Road 'Hall' No.5970 *Hengrave Hall* negotiating the permanent way slack around Bayston Hill with an up Class 'E' freight on 24th September 1960, still with nearly seven months to go before she got her next (and final) Heavy General overhaul. Her train was still representative of the former era, with a mixture of open and covered wagons, the railways still having some impact on the conveyance of general and industrial merchandise. Signs of quarrying at Sharpstone Hill are evident on the left.

MICHAEL MENSING

Canton 'Grange' No.6859 *Yiewsley Grange* climbing past Bayston Hill on 24th September 1960 with a southbound goods, probably an express freight from either Saltney or Coton Hill to Cardiff. At this time, a pair of Canton 'Granges' were rostered for return overnight services between Pengam, Saltney and Margam over this route, but this could have been the 4.10 p.m. Saltney to Pontypool Road, part of a Canton '73XXX' diagram. In two months, the engine would go into Swindon for a heavy general repair, and would emerge in pristine condition to continue on Canton's Class '5' turns.

MICHAEL MENSING

There was a good variety of both power and trains on this section of the line out of Shrewsbury. Here, ex-LMS Fowler 2-6-4T No.42307, now based at Landore, was passing Bayston Hill on 24th September 1960 with the 2.50 p.m. Shrewsbury to Swansea Victoria, which would join the Central Wales line beyond Craven Arms. The four-coach corridor set rostered for this train had worked up that morning as the 10.25 a.m. Swansea, but the tight turnround at Shrewsbury prevented the train engine from doing the same. No.42307 had been stationed at Swansea (Paxton St.) for these services until July 1955, but had moved west to Neyland, returning in September 1959. When Paxton St. closed – in that month – the passenger engines went to Landore, and the freight to Llanelly.

MICHAEL MENSING

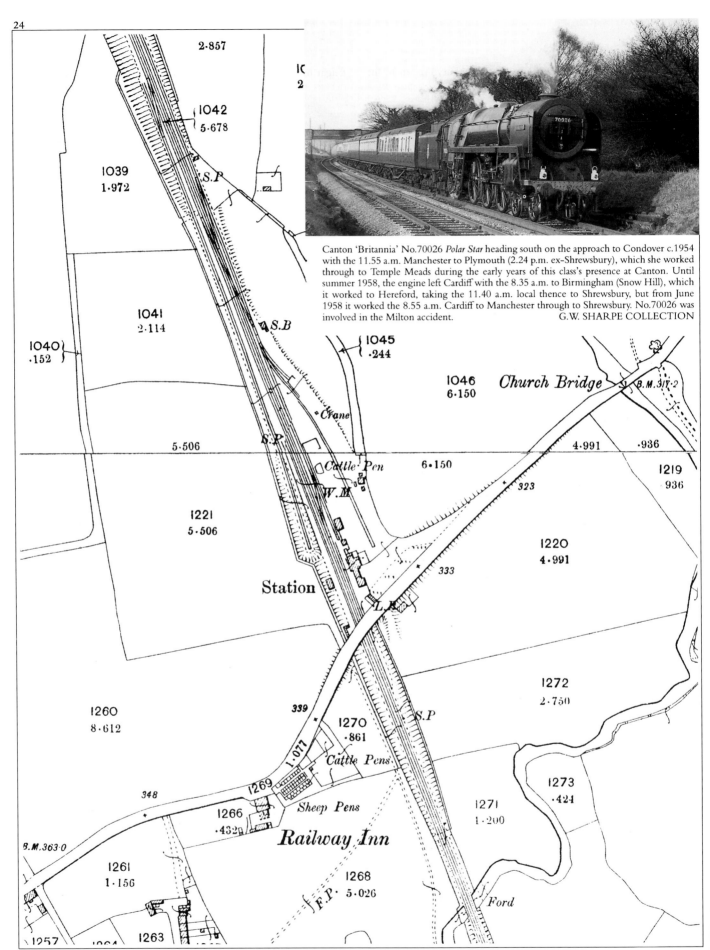

2·857

1042
5·678

1039
1·972

S.P

1041
2·114

S.B

1040
·152

1045
·244

1046
6·150

Church Bridge

B.M.317·2

5·506

Crane

S.P

4·991   ·936

1219
·936

Cattle Pen

6·150

323

W.M

1221
5·506

1220
4·991

333

Station

L.B

1272
2·750

1260
8·612

339

S.P

1·077

1270
·861

1·200

1271
1·200

1273
·424

Cattle Pens

1269

348

1266
·432

Sheep Pens

B.M.363·0

Railway Inn

1261
1·156

1268
F.P. 5·026

1257   1263

Ford

Canton 'Britannia' No.70026 *Polar Star* heading south on the approach to Condover c.1954 with the 11.55 a.m. Manchester to Plymouth (2.24 p.m. ex-Shrewsbury), which she worked through to Temple Meads during the early years of this class's presence at Canton. Until summer 1958, the engine left Cardiff with the 8.35 a.m. to Birmingham (Snow Hill), which it worked to Hereford, taking the 11.40 a.m. local thence to Shrewsbury, but from June 1958 it worked the 8.55 a.m. Cardiff to Manchester through to Shrewsbury. No.70026 was involved in the Milton accident.   G.W. SHARPE COLLECTION

Taken from Ordnance Survey for 1902. (Crown copyright reserved)

CONDOVER

Condover was the first station south of Shrewsbury (4m 26ch) and had slightly-staggered Up and Down Platforms, with a signal box at the north end of the Down Platform. An 1886 map shows a Down Refuge Siding to the north of the station, with a short yard siding outside it and a spur serving a loading dock and cattle pen behind the signal box.

In July 1941, the Down Refuge Siding was lengthened and converted into a Down Loop, whilst on the opposite side of the running lines, an Up Loop was constructed. These were conveniently located to support the loops beyond Bayston Hill box for holding freight traffic destined for or originating from Shrewsbury, and in the case of the Down, to allow freight to clear the main lines to await a clear passage up the bank to Dorrington, Leebotwood or beyond.

The yard siding was removed in 1961, whilst the Loops, each of which had a capacity of engine, 65 wagons and a brake van, were taken out of use in 1966, along with the loading bay spur.

Condover station was closed to passengers on 9th June 1958, whilst the signal box was closed in May 1967 with the implementation of MAS.

The approach road to Condover station, seen a few years after the closure to passengers. The main station buildings, which included living accommodation, were situated on the east (Down) side of the line, a half-mile or so from the village.
MIKE LEWIS

Condover station looking north, again after closure, showing the station buildings, signal box, and Down Loop and spur. The platforms had been removed soon after closure in 1958, but the goods loops and box survived until 1966/7.
MIKE LEWIS

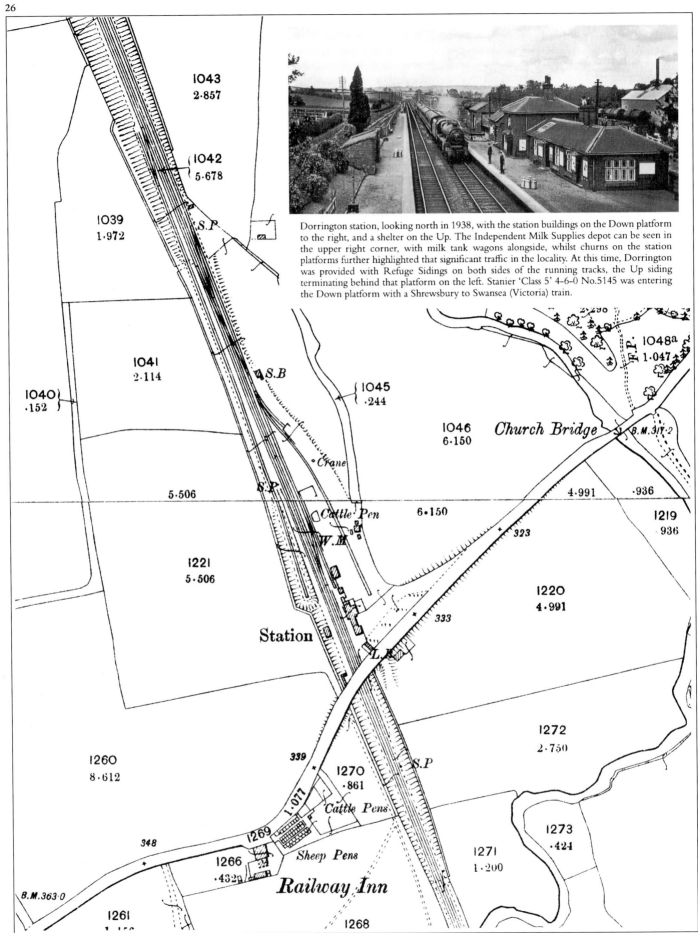

26

1043
2·857

1042
5·678

1039
1·972

S.P.

1041
2·114

1040
·152

S.B

1045
·244

Crane

S.P.

5·506

Cattle Pen

W.M

1221
5·506

1046
6·150

Church Bridge

B.M.317·2

4·991

·936

6·150

323

1219
·936

1220
4·991

333

Station

L.B

1272
2·750

1260
8·612

339

1270
·861

S.P

1·077

1269

Cattle Pens

348

1266
·432

Sheep Pens

Railway Inn

1273
·424

1271
1·200

B.M.363·0

1261

1268

1048a
1·047

F.P.

Dorrington station, looking north in 1938, with the station buildings on the Down platform to the right, and a shelter on the Up. The Independent Milk Supplies depot can be seen in the upper right corner, with milk tank wagons alongside, whilst churns on the station platforms further highlighted that significant traffic in the locality. At this time, Dorrington was provided with Refuge Sidings on both sides of the running tracks, the Up siding terminating behind that platform on the left. Stanier 'Class 5' 4-6-0 No.5145 was entering the Down platform with a Shrewsbury to Swansea (Victoria) train.

Taken from 25-inch Ordnance Survey for 1902. Crown copyright reserved.

DORRINGTON

The station forecourt at Dorrington after closure to passenger traffic, illustrating the quite substantial buildings provided on the Down side. The cart weighbridge in the foreground may well have been much used by the station's milk traffic.
MIKE LEWIS

Dorrington station (at 6m 34ch) was two miles south of Condover, and became a centre for cattle and milk traffic. In 1886. the station had two platforms, and a single goods yard line to the north, on the east (down) side of the main line, with trailing connections to each running line. This yard also served two loading banks (for livestock) and a short siding via a wagon turntable at its southern end, close to the northern end of the Down platform. The goods line was extended northwards beyond the yard to form a refuge siding (capacity of engine, 46 wagons and van), with its own connection to the Down Main.

The station signal box was located in the goods yard, some 200 yards north of the platforms.

An Up Refuge Siding was added in 1889, on the opposite side of the main lines to the goods yard; this had a capacity of 41 wagons, engine and van.

By 1902, the Down side had been remodelled. The wagon turn-table had been removed, with a single cattle pen on the spur near the Down platform. A pair of dead-end sidings were added behind the existing yard, leaving the original siding to the south of the signal box; the inner siding was of some length, probably for mileage traffic, whilst the outer was short, leading to an end-loading bank. At around the same time, the Up platform was extended at its northern end.

Dorrington was well known for the conveyance of milk from its early years in a modest way, but a dairy was established there in 1921 by Midland Farmers Ltd., alongside the goods yard. As well as delivering the cooled milk locally, this company also despatched churns via Shrewsbury to Paddington, but by the early 'thirties Midland Farmers was in financial difficulties, and the concern was offered to the Milk Marketing Board. In 1935, the depot ended up in the hands of Independent Milk Supplies.

The IMS company had just opened a new depot at Rossmore Road, Marylebone, alongside the ex-Great Central's main line, which possessed a rail connection. It was already receiving milk from its other depot, at Sanquhar (Dumfries), and planned to operate a similar service from Dorrington using 3,000- gallon, six-wheel tanks, which were ready for traffic by the summer of 1936. Thus, in that year, the short outer siding was extended into a private siding for Independent Milk Supplies.

Dorrington, again looking north, showing the site after closure and platform removal. The milk depot can again be seen in the background, possibly at this time still in the hands of IMS, or otherwise Newhall Dairies (from late 1961).
MIKE LEWIS

The daily journey to Marylebone was quite a circuitous one, running firstly to Shrewsbury, then up the Great Western main line to Banbury, where the short train of tanks and a passenger brake van was handed over to the L&NE. The train was then taken north-eastwards to Woodford Halse, then along the former Great Central main line to the IMS depot at Marylebone. The empties followed this route in reverse. After Nationalisation, the trains ran direct from Banbury via the Bicester line to Marylebone.

In January 1942, the Down Refuge siding was converted into a loop with a capacity of 65 wagons in addition to engine and van, one of the series of four on the 11½-mile climb between Bayston Hill box and the summit beyond Church Stretton. It was cut back again and stop blocked in 1959, again becoming a Down Refuge siding.

Dorrington station closed to passengers on 9th June 1958, but railway goods facilities remained until 1965.

Insofar as the milk siding was concerned, the dairy became the property of Newhall Dairies Ltd. in 1961, and United Dairies in 1965.

The Up Refuge siding, which latterly ran partly behind the Up Platform, remained in use until 1964. The Down side layout was remodelled again in 1976 to provide a single trailing connection from the Down Main for the yard.

8·753

177
4·603

M.P.

176
1·340

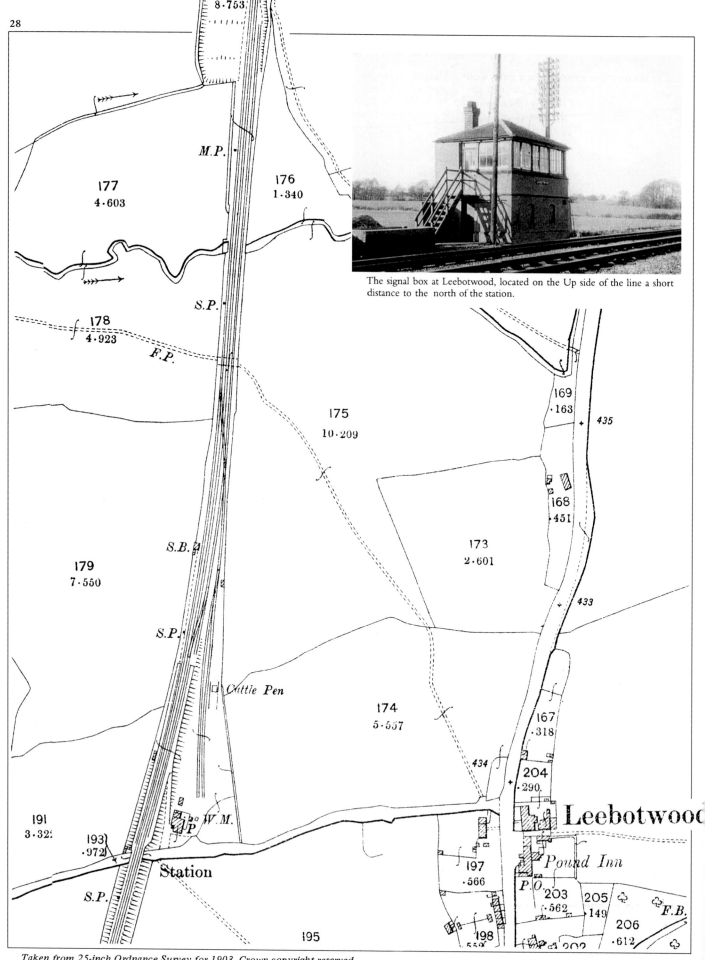

The signal box at Leebotwood, located on the Up side of the line a short distance to the north of the station.

S.P.

178
4·923

F.P.

175
10·209

169
·163

435

168
·451

179
7·550

S.B.

173
2·601

433

S.P.

Cattle Pen

174
5·557

167
·318

434

204
·290

191
3·32

193)
·972

P
W.M.

Station

Leebotwood

S.P.

197
·566

Pound Inn

P.O.

203
·562

205
·149

F.B.

206
·612

195

198
·55

202

LEEBOTWOOD

The station at Leebotwood was 3 miles south of Dorrington, at 9m 23ch. A map for 1886 shows Up and Down platforms of equal length, originally with a signal box at the north end of the Up platform, though this had been closed in 1872 and renewed a little further to the north centrally to the yard connections out on the main line.

There was a Down Refuge siding to the north of the station on the eastern side of the running lines, the southern part of which provided access from the goods yard's two loop sidings onto the Down Main. At the station end of the goods sidings was a wagon turntable, whilst a cattle pen was located on the easternmost loop. There was also a trailing connection across to the Up Main from the two sidings.

With the increase in traffic levels, the platforms were both extended northwards in 1887, as was the refuge siding access. The yard sidings were remodelled to become two independent dead-end roads around the turn of the century.

The Down Refuge siding became a Down Goods loop in 1941 to accommodate the heavy wartime traffic, but, as at Dorrington, it was reduced to a refuge siding again in 1959.

Leebotwood station closed to passengers on 9th June 1958, with closure of goods facilities at the same time. The yard was lifted in 1961 and the signal box was closed in October 1967, with the advent of MAS.

No.6812 *Enborne Grange* heading south through Leebotwood with a Down class 'C' freight on 27th May 1959. The engine was stationed at Pontypool Road, and was probably working back to its home shed with a fast freight from either Saltney or Shrewsbury.
BRIAN PENNEY

A Canton 'Britannia' coasting down the bank from Church Stretton at the head of the lightweight 11.50 a.m. Swansea to Manchester service on 27th May 1959, with a run of around fifteen minutes to her call at Shrewsbury. After a one-hour turn round, she was due to return to Cardiff with the 2.55 p.m. Manchester train, usually a fourteen-coach service with sections from Glasgow, Manchester and Liverpool for Cardiff and Plymouth, the latter detached at Pontypool Road.
BRIAN PENNEY

Working hard on the climb to Church Stretton, Shrewsbury 'Castle' No.5097 *Sarum Castle* was on the first leg of the double-home working (Salop 50) to Newton Abbot with the 9.10 a.m. Liverpool to Plymouth on Whit Monday 10th June 1957. Although Coleham's 'Castles' worked mostly to Bristol with the daily North & West services at this time, this diagram ran through to Newton, whilst a weekend duty visited Plymouth.

MICHAEL MENSING

Against the backdrop of Shropshire foothills, Longsight unrebuilt 'Patriot' No.45520 *Llandudno* was working the 8.55 a.m. Cardiff to Manchester at Dudgeley Mill on 10th June 1957. This train had been worked from Cardiff to Hereford by a Canton 'Britannia' (on Turn 11), which then returned to Cardiff. From summer 1958, a Canton 'Britannia' (Turn 5) was working the 8.55 a.m. Cardiff through to Shrewsbury, returning with the 2.24 p.m.

MICHAEL MENSING

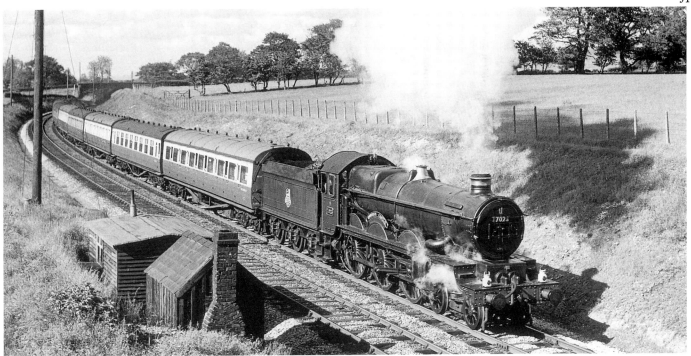

Climbing the 1 in 100 at Dudgeley Mill, one of Canton's best 'Castles' – No.7023 *Penrice Castle* – is seen with the 2.55 p.m. Manchester to Cardiff (5.5 p.m. ex-Shrewsbury) on Whit Monday, 10th June 1957. The train was comprised of former company stock, probably in its 'Carmine & Cream' livery (though the 'Maroon' was being applied by this time), with coaches from both Manchester and Liverpool to Cardiff. Ordinarily, this train also conveyed through coaches for Plymouth and Penzance at the rear – detached at Pontypool Road – but on busier days the train ran in two parts, with the Cardiff portion usually leading. No.7023 went new to Canton in July 1949 and remained there until August 1960 when, in the move that took 'Kings' to Canton, she was transferred to Worcester who, not surprisingly, held on to her until withdrawn in June 1964. In the background is the B4370 overbridge, carrying the road to join the main A49 off to the right; this trunk route closely followed the railway through the Strettons.
MICHAEL MENSING

THE STRETTONS

In its climb from Shrewsbury, the S&H route encountered its highest point on the route as it ran through the Strettons, with a final lift to the summit of around 600ft above mean sea level, occurring after a short stretch of level ground through and to the south of Church Stretton station. This involved an almost continuous climb of nearly 450ft over the 14 miles from Shrewsbury station, with the summit near the occupation overbridge close to the site of the old Castle, at a point where the valley was at its narrowest. Through the valley, the railway was accompanied closely by the modern A49 trunk road (the old Roman Watling Street, upgraded to form a bypass to the Strettons), whilst the former main road (later the B4370) wended its way through All, Church and Little Strettons. A feature of this section was the number of road overbridges across the railway that either carried the B road itself, or those roads and lanes connecting it with the A49: there were eight over the 3½-mile length.

ALL STRETTON
COMLEY ROAD

As it approached the village of All Stretton, the railway passed beneath the B4370, then shortly afterwards ran under the Comley Road, with Dudgeley Mill beyond on the west side of the line. This part of the line was on a climb of 1 in 100 from Shrewsbury, and heralded a section of outstanding natural beauty.

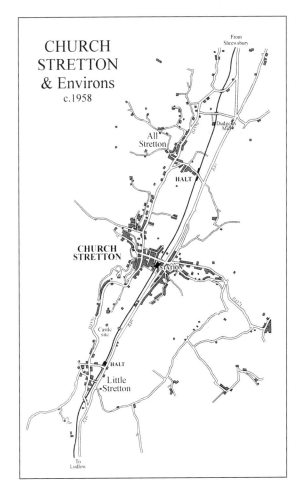

CHURCH STRETTON & Environs c.1958

From Shrewsbury

Dudgeley Mill

All Stretton

HALT

CHURCH STRETTON

Castle site

HALT

Little Stretton

To Ludlow

Descending the 1 in 100 at Dudgeley Mill (seen to the right of the train), against a backdrop of the towering, beautiful Shropshire landscape, Longsight 'Jubilee' No.45587 *Baroda*, with Fowler tender, is seen on a train of ex–Great Western stock on Whit Monday, 10th June 1957. The engine was working through from Pontypool Road on the 7.30 a.m. Penzance to Manchester, with the regular portion of the train fully roof-boarded. The leading Brake Compo and Dining Car worked from Plymouth to Manchester, and alternated daily between WR and LMR stock, but the remainder was scheduled for WR coaches, comprising the five-coach Penzance to Manchester set following the diner, and, in this instance, the strengthening vehicles at the rear. The contrast in scenery to the north and south of Dudgeley Mill overbridge is well illustrated in this sequence of photographs
MICHAEL MENSING

ALL STRETTON HALT

In the Winter 1956 service, still in force at this time, Canton Turn 12 worked the 8.35 a.m. Cardiff to Birmingham as far as Hereford, and then continued with the 11.40 a.m. local to Shrewsbury, rather a waste of Class '7' power, though necessary to get the engine to Shrewsbury. The return was with the 2.24 p.m. Shrewsbury (11.45 a.m. Manchester) to Bristol. Here, on Whit Monday, 10th June 1957, Britannia No.70028 *Royal Star* was passing All Stretton Halt with the 11.40 a.m. local service from Hereford.
MICHAEL MENSING

This short-platformed halt stood some three-quarters-of-a-mile to the south of the Comley Road bridge, at 11m 57ch from Shrewsbury, and was opened in February 1936. The platforms were served by paths from the sides of Farm Lane bridge (which road ran eastwards from the centre of the village), and were staggered; the Up platform to the north of the bridge, and the Down to the south, whilst each had a small wooden shelter and a sign. The halt was closed on 9th June 1958, along with many other stations on this part of the route.

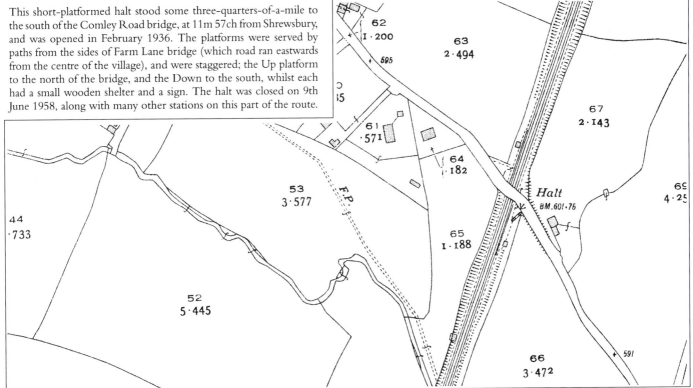

Taken from Ordnance Survey for 1903. (Crown copyright reserved)

A regular duty for a Banbury 'Hall', the three-coach 4.20 p.m. Hereford to Shrewsbury local, is seen passing All Stretton Halt non-stop with No.5930 *Hannington Hall* in charge, on Monday, 10th June 1957. Having brought the Marylebone milk empties from Banbury to Shrewsbury early that morning, the engine then took the 1.15 p.m. Shrewsbury to Hereford local, and the 4.20 p.m. back. It returned to Banbury that night with the 8.5 p.m. Dorrington to Marylebone milk. This duty was worked by Banbury and Coleham engines on alternate days, and on a Monday would usually be a Shrewsbury engine, although the Bank Holiday engine arrangements doubtless called for adjustments. New in June 1933, No.5930 went to Banbury in June 1935 and remained there until November 1959.
MICHAEL MENSING

An unusual working on Whit Monday, 10th June 1957, with Canton Standard 'Class 4' No.75022 working the 5.30 p.m. Shrewsbury to Swansea Victoria past All Stretton Halt. Canton 'Class 4s' worked daily into Hereford with a morning passenger from Cardiff, and the engine had doubtless been 'borrowed' for the duty, which is believed to have been normally worked by a Paxton Street 2-6-4T.
MICHAEL MENSING

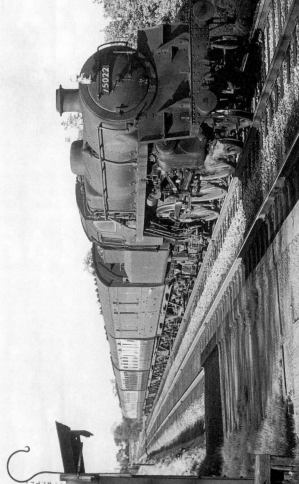

The 3.55 p.m. local passenger from Shrewsbury to Hereford approaching All Stretton Halt on Whit Monday 10th June 1957, powered by Longsight 'Jubilee' No.45689 *Ajax*. Four ex-Great Western coaches formed the train, with Brake Seconds sandwiching a Compo and Second, This train was one of only two down (and one up) that called at the halt each day, allowing residents to visit Shrewsbury on a morning train (7.56 a.m.) and return on an afternoon or early evening service. In view of the 'one-coach' platform, they would probably be required to travel in a specific vehicle. MICHAEL MENSING

Coleham's '5MT' No.45406 drifting downhill through All Stretton's tiny up platform with the 12.25 p.m. Swansea Victoria to Shrewsbury on Whit Monday, 10th June 1957. This was the usual return working of the noon train from Shrewsbury the previous weekday. Shrewsbury's '5MTs' still worked mainly over their traditional routes to Crewe, Manchester and Liverpool, as well as to Hereford, and to Swansea over the Central Wales line. MICHAEL MENSING

CHURCH STRETTON

The original Church Stretton station stood (at 12m 58ch) to the north side of the road bridge, with the main station building on the west (town) side of the lines. The up (northbound) platform was shorter than the down in order to accommodate the trailing connection from the Down Main into the goods yard, on the west side of the running lines. This led across to a wagon turntable on the edge of the cattle pens (two faces), with spurs for loading and unloading. The goods yard originally had two loop sidings parallel to the main line, with a second wagon turntable linking the outermost siding with the goods shed, and a third (dead-end) siding around the back of the shed, for mileage purposes.

Another siding, to the outside of the mileage road, was added in 1913, and designated an Up Refuge siding. On the down side, there was a Down Refuge siding with a short spur at the south end of the platform. Church Stretton signal box was located between the end of this spur and the north end of the down platform.

In May 1914. a new passenger station was opened immediately to the south of the road bridge (at 12m 63ch), with platforms of equal length. In the goods yard, the Victorian wagon turntables were removed, the cattle pen accommodation and loading bank being on a single spur, whilst the goods shed was rebuilt and provided with its own dead-end road.

As part of wartime improvements along the section, the Down Refuge Siding was lengthened at the north end and connected into the Down Main to become a Down Goods loop, becoming operational in September 1941.

Goods services were withdrawn from Church Stretton in September 1966, though a spur from the Up Main to the loading bank was retained for a while. The Up Refuge siding was taken out of use in 1969.

Shrewsbury Class '5MT' No.45143 restarting the 10.25 a.m. Swansea Victoria to Shrewsbury under the road bridge and away from Church Stretton (due 1.46 p.m.) on the falling incline towards All Stretton on 10th June 1957. Church Stretton was usually the only intermediate call for Swansea trains between Craven Arms and Shrewsbury, though some Saturday fast services ran through non-stop from Knighton or Craven Arms, sometimes with services extended to Manchester. The old station buildings can be seen in the left foreground, whilst the loading bay and cattle dock are seen ahead of the engine, with the goods shed beyond.

MICHAEL MENSING

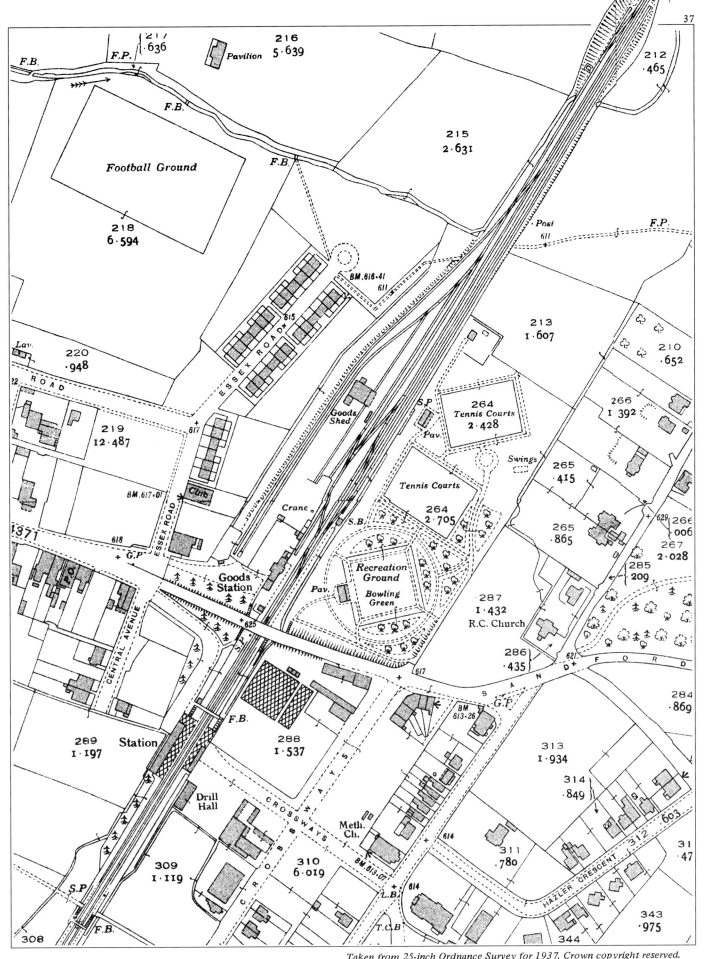

F.B.

F.P.

F.B.

217
·636

216
5·639   Pavilion

Football Ground

218
6·594

215
2·631

212
·465

F.B.

F.P.

Post
611

213
1·607

210
·652

BM.616·41
611

Lav.

220
·948

ESSEX ROAD

615

266
1·392

ROAD

219
12·487

617

S.P.

264
Tennis Courts
2·428

Pav.

Swings

265
·415

BM.617·01   Club

Goods
Shed

Tennis Courts

264
2·705

265
·865

266
·006

Crane

ESSEX ROAD

S.B.

267
2·028

285
209

1371

618

+ G.P.

Goods
Station

Recreation
Ground
Bowling
Green

Pav.

287
1·432
R.C. Church

286
·435

621

629

CENTRAL AVENUE

P.O.

+ 625

617

S AND FORD

G.P.

284
·869

S.P.

F.B.

288
1·537

BM
613·26

313
1·934

289
1·197   Station

CROSSWAYS

314
·849

603

312

31
·47

Drill
Hall

Meth.
Ch.

614

311
·780

343
·975

S.P.

309
1·119

310
6·019

BM.613·07

614

HAZLER CRESCENT

L.B.

344

308

F.B.

T.C.B.

Church Stretton station c.1950, looking south towards Hereford. The station was rebuilt in the years before the Great War: the proposal was first reported in 1911, building work was under way in 1912 and completed by May 1914, when the new station was opened. The platforms were rebuilt entirely to the south of the road bridge, and were thus now separated from the goods yard at the north end by the road bridge. 'Standard' station buildings with overall canopies were provided, along with a connecting footbridge.

LENS OF SUTTON

An Abergavenny-based ex-L & NW 0-8-0 steaming under the road bridge at the north end of Church Stretton station with a southbound class 'H' freight during 1953. These engines were a common sight north of Abergavenny, both on general freight, and on banking duties between Abergavenny (Monmouth Road) and Llanvihangel. Abergavenny shed housed nine of these engines at this time, and others were regularly to be found over this part of the North & West route from Coleham and Swansea (Paxton St.). The '124½' milepost can be seen below the station nameboard, measured from Shrewsbury.

RUSSELL MULFORD

An evening express to Cardiff – possibly a special – passing Church Stretton on Whit Monday, 10th June 1957 behind Shrewsbury Caprotti Class '5' No.73134 with a 14-coach train.   MICHAEL MENSING

On Whit Monday, 10th June 1957, Chester 'Modified Hall' No.7922 *Salford Hall* is seen running non-stop on the half-mile of level track through Church Stretton station with the 4.15 p.m. Cardiff to Birkenhead service, which the engine worked through to Chester. She would shortly start the almost continuous twelve-mile descent into Coleham. The latticework footbridge to the south of the platforms carried a public footpath across the line.   MICHAEL MENSING

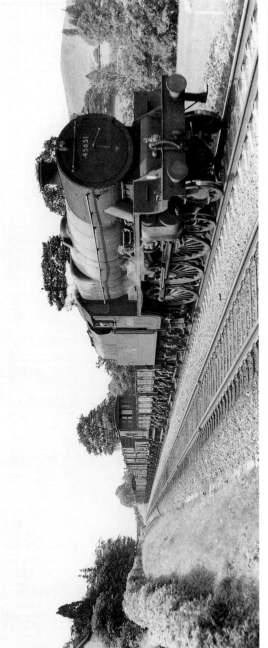

Dropping down the short section of 1 in 150 from the summit after the long climb from Bromfield, Shrewsbury's 'Jubilee' No.45651 *Showell* was approaching the half-mile section of level track leading into Church Stretton station with a Class 'H' ('8') goods service for Shrewsbury on Friday, 10th August 1962. The occupation overbridge leading to the old castle site can be seen in the distance, near the summit.　　　　　　　　DEREK CROSS

Ebbw Junction '28XX' 2-8-0 No.3807 standing in the Down Refuge Loop, just to the north of the road bridge at Church Stretton station with a southbound class 'E' freight, probably for the Newport area, on 10th August 1962. This loop could take an engine, 65 wagons and a van, adequate for a non-banked, 28XX-hauled train on the gradients up from Dorrington; for most of the services, there was a 60-wagon limit in any event. There was also an Up Refuge Siding, and this, unusually, terminated around the back of the goods shed. No.3807 was a long term Ebbw Jct. engine, first going there in January 1942 and remaining until withdrawn in 1965.
DEREK CROSS

In September 1962, Canton shed closed for steam locomotives, and its allocation was moved to Cardiff East Dock shed. About a month before that move, on 10th August 1962, Canton 'Castle' No.5092 *Tresco Abbey* was seen approaching Church Stretton with the heavy 11.50 a.m. Swansea to Manchester (M68). This was her last full year of service; she was withdrawn in July 1963.
DEREK CROSS

The second-ever double-chimneyed 'Castle', No.4090 *Dorchester Castle*, heading southwards out of Church Stretton station with the 9.5 a.m. Manchester (Piccadilly) to Paignton service (Train V92) on Friday, 10th August 1962. This train was formed of eight Eastern Region coaches with an articulated pair on the front. No.4090 had spent three months in store prior to being temporarily transferred to Coleham for the summer service in early July, and would briefly return to store in September prior to being sent to Cardiff East Dock for her final allocation.
DEREK CROSS

Jubilee No.45660 *Rooke* approaching the occupation bridge near the castle site to the south of Church Stretton with a Shrewsbury to Swansea Victoria service on 24th April 1964. The Long Mynd Hotel, on the south-western outskirts of Church Stretton, is prominent in the top left-hand corner; built in 1901 as a spa (with imported water from Llandrindod), this was used as a St. Dunstan's centre during the Second World War; it had seen much of the traffic development on the North & West route   DEREK CROSS

Cardiff 'East Dock 'Hall' No.5962 *Wantage Hall* was photographed from the occupation bridge three-quarters-of-a-mile to the south of Church Stretton station with a down excursion '1X86' on 10th August 1964, looking north. She was withdrawn in November of that year from Worcester shed.
                     DEREK CROSS

CASTLE OCCUPATION BRIDGE

At the end of the level, straight section from Church Stretton station, the line climbed briefly to the summit, passing underneath the overbridge leading to the hillock that carried the site of the old Castle (and the cemetery) as it did so.

A 'Castle' is here pictured heading south at speed under the occupation bridge between Church Stretton and Little Stretton on Monday, 6th June 1955. The locomotive was carrying number 227, which identified the 8.20 a.m. Cardiff to Manchester (Mayfield); this may have been its outbound working. The scheduled return for that working was the 12.0 noon Manchester to Cardiff, which was probably be the service seen here. The up distant for Church Stretton box is seen against the bridge, with a PW hut in front.
RUSSELL MULFORD

Pontypool Road 'Grange' No.6810 *Blakemere Grange* making hard work of the run between Little Stretton and Church Stretton with a northbound Class 'E' ('6') freight composed of containers, vans and coal traffic on 10th August 1962. This was the summit of the climb from Ludlow, which culminated in a 1½-mile section of 1 in 112.
DEREK CROSS

Stanier '8F' 2-8-0 No.48409 nearing the occupation bridge on 24th April 1964 with a northbound fitted Class 'D' ('5') freight, probably off the Central Wales line as the first five wagons were carrying cattle. The engine was from Llanelly shed, though it would shortly move to Bath (Green Park). This type of freight required that not less than one third of the automatic brakes on the vehicles were operative.   DEREK CROSS

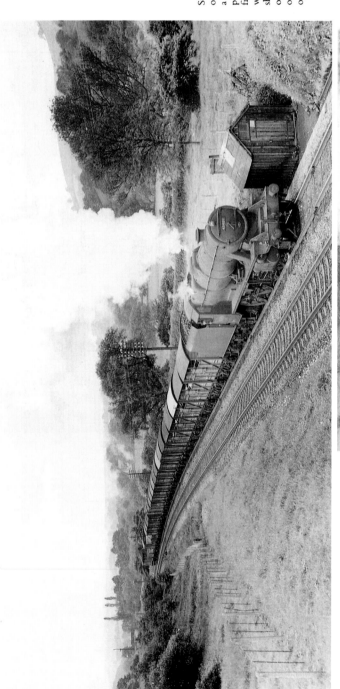

A long way from home, Wellingborough's Stanier '8F' 2-8-0 No.48492 heading a short Class 'H' ('8') freight composed mostly of wagons of coal on the approach to the occupation bridge on 12th April 1964. The site of the former Little Stretton Halt is marked by the tall poplar trees and overbridge in the distance.   DEREK CROSS

Yet another 'Hall' in charge of a through West to North early summer extra, this time the 8.5 a.m. Paignton to Manchester heading towards the occupation bridge on 6th June 1955. Probably used on freight working during the week, and pressed into passenger use at busy holiday periods, it was little wonder timekeeping went so awry on most weekends. The position of the nearby A49 trunk road is shown by the huts above the locomotive.

RUSSELL MULFORD

The Canton shine is evident on this 'Castle' at the head of the 12.38 p.m. Cardiff to Manchester (Exchange) on the approach to the occupation bridge on 6th June 1955, with ex-L & NE stock in evidence. There was a major change in the train numbering system of North & West services for the summer of 1955 to allow the same number to be carried for the passage over both LMR and WR metals, and the traditional GWR consecutive numbering arrangements for relief trains were abandoned in the district.

RUSSELL MULFORD

Pictured a little way to the north of the site of Little Stretton Halt, Shrewsbury 'Hall' No.6934 *Beachamwell Hall* was heading a short southbound class 'H' ('8') goods through the picturesque countryside on 24th April 1964. By this time, the surviving 'Halls' were largely in use on freight duties, though sheds away from the West Country still diagrammed them for passenger work, mostly on local trains.

DEREK CROSS

Llanelly Stanier '8F' 2-8-0 No.48706 running through the Shropshire countryside with a southbound Class 'E' ('6') freight on the approach to Little Stretton Halt in June 1964. This would probably have been destined for the Central Wales line, with the load including coal, possibly timber baulks, and oil tankers.

DEREK CROSS

Paxton Street Fowler 'Class 4' 2-6-4T No.42390 heading south on the approach to Little Stretton Halt with a six-coach 2.40 p.m. Shrewsbury to Swansea Central Wales relief service in July 1955. These services were usually of four or five coaches, but an additional vehicle (perhaps the ex-GW coach in the middle of the train) had been added for this busy day. The Central Wales trains did not call at the halt.

RUSSELL MULFORD

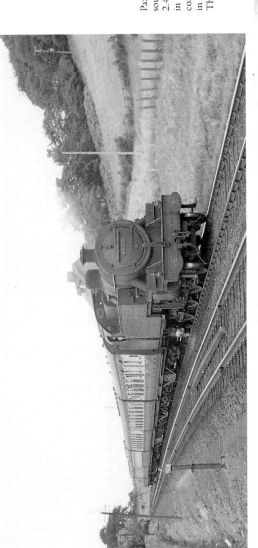

A Southall 'Hall' heading north through Little Stretton Halt with the 10.4 a.m. Exeter to Manchester (London Road) on 6th June 1955. This service was scheduled for a ten-coach train with just a pair of Composites in the centre, obviously catering for the holiday trade. The stock actually started from Exminster at 9.18 a.m., but unlike the 9.5 a.m. Paignton that it preceded, this train served Temple Meads. Southall 'Halls' were often seen at peak periods on the North & West with passenger trains, having invariably worked a freight into the West of England or South Wales the day before.

RUSSELL MULFORD

The 11.15 a.m. Swansea to Manchester was worked from Cardiff to Shrewsbury by a Canton 'Britannia', and No.70027 *Rising Star* is seen here on 6th June 1955 with that service. The train had just passed through Little Stretton Halt, with its beautiful countryside behind. The first three coaches were attached at Cardiff General station with the engine, with the regular five-coach Swansea portion behind them. The rear vehicles were removed at Stockport.
                                                RUSSELL MULFORD

Shrewsbury '8F' 2-8-0 No.48706 on passenger duty, possibly with the 1.10 p.m. Llandilo to Shrewsbury (Central Wales) service, passing Little Stretton in June 1955. The tall poplar trees at the halt were visible for a considerable distance from either side, as trees and foliage close to the railway were kept well trimmed down by the PW department to minimise the possibility of lineside fires.
                                                RUSSELL MULFORD

LITTLE STRETTON HALT

Opened in April 1935, the halt (at 14m 0ch) was located off Elms Lane, which ran eastwards to the A49 from the northern part of the village. The platforms were both to the north of the bridge, with accesses to the side, and each was provided with a timber shelter and nameboard.

Around the turn of the century, a small signal box was opened a hundred yards or so to the north of the road bridge on the down side (at 13m 56ch), though its operation seems to have been on an intermittent basis from around the Great War, and it effectively closed in the mid-1920s. However, its total closure was not recorded until the early 1930s, when it ceased to appear in service books.

The halt was closed in June 1958.

Little Stretton Halt was located against the north face of the north-ernmost road bridge connecting the village with the A49 trunk road, and was of timber construction. Just 1¼ miles from Church Stretton station, the halt was served by eight Shrewsbury & Hereford local trains daily in the late 1930s. This official view, taken on 6th November 1935, shows the basic facilities on the down platform, with an LMS timetable ('Main Line, Crewe & Carlisle') adorning the interior side wall. Ragleth Hill forms the backdrop to this scene.
NATIONAL RAILWAY MUSEUM

A panoramic view of the halt and the breathtaking scenery surrounding it, seen on 6th November 1935, looking north. The occupation bridge can just be seen in the far distance, with the Church Stretton distant signal in front. The Long Mynd forms the backdrop to the west (left), with the houses of Worldsend in its foothills
NATIONAL RAILWAY MUSEUM

Newton Abbot 'Castle' No.5078 *Beaufort* passing through Little Stretton Halt with the 8.0 a.m. Plymouth to Liverpool (with a through coach to Glasgow Central at the head) and 8.5 a.m. coaches from Kingswear to Manchester, combined at Newton Abbot during the winter timetable. This was the first leg of the double home working to Shrewsbury for the Newton engine and crew, on Monday, 10th June 1957. The roof board shows the BR standard 'West of England Bristol Shrewsbury & Liverpool (Lime Street)' legend, adopted because through coaches between major LMR stations and the West Country often had different points of destination and origin in the latter within a return working, although it was not the case in this instance.

MICHAEL MENSING

No.5097 *Sarum Castle* having passed under Elms Lane road bridge and heading through Little Stretton Halt with the 8.45 a.m. Plymouth. This train had much the same formation throughout the 1950s, as motor vehicles had not yet made heavy inroads into the railway's holiday traffic.
RUSSELL MULFORD

Canton 'Britannia' No.70028 *Royal Star* with the 11.45 a.m. Manchester to Plymouth passing Little Stretton Halt on 10th June 1957, in this case working through from Shrewsbury to Bristol, after which it would work the 7.15 p.m. Bristol to Pontypool Road (12 noon Penzance to Crewe) and the 11.35 p.m. thence to Cardiff. The A49 trunk road was just beyond the railway fencing at this point, on the low embankment.
MICHAEL MENSING

Heading away from Crown Lane bridge, Little Stretton, Coleham shed Standard 'Class 5MT' 4-6-0 No.73025 bringing the four-coach 12.20 p.m. Swansea to Shrewsbury (Central Wales) service towards the halt on Saturday, 25th April 1964. The next stop of this class 'A' train was Church Stretton on Saturdays, though non-stop to Shrewsbury on weekdays.
DEREK CROSS

No.5097 *Sarum Castle* was a top 'Castle' at Shrewsbury at this time, having been received back from a Heavy Intermediate repair at Swindon in February 1955, and was entrusted with the double-home working to Newton Abbot in June 1955. She is pictured here with the 8.45 a.m. (Saturdays-only) Plymouth to Crewe, passing under Crown Lane on the approach to Little Stretton Halt; her train contained vehicles for Liverpool at the head, and Manchester (including, dining car) at the rear.
RUSSELL MULFORD

CROWN LANE

Crown Lane ran eastwards from the centre of the village to the A49, and crossed over the railway at a point very close to the trunk road. It had good views northwards to the Elms Lane bridge (and halt), and southwards to the Ludlow Road bridge.

This July 1961 view of train 'V98' heading south through Little Stretton was taken from Crown Lane bridge, looking north, The train was the 3.30 p.m. Manchester (Piccadilly) to Plymouth, with Canton 'Grange' No.6833 *Calcot Grange* possibly working through to Bristol.
RUSSELL MULFORD

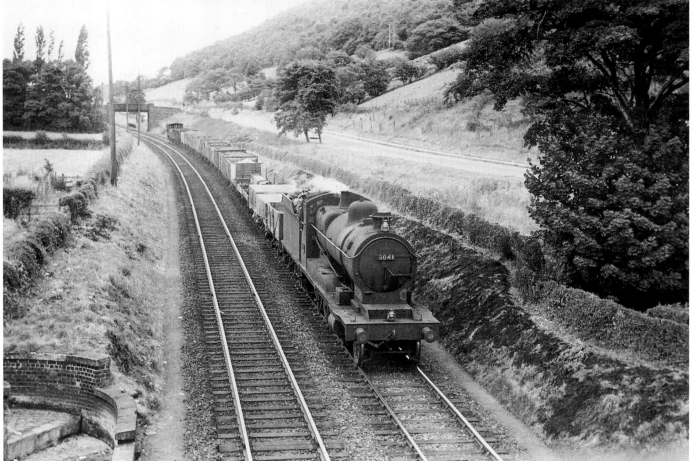

'RODs' were a common sight along the North & West route in the 1950s and here Coleham's No.3041 was heading a short Class 'H' freight as it neared Crown Lane bridge, Little Stretton, in June 1955. Within a year, just ten of the class were still in traffic, with No.3041 surviving until March 1958. Little Stretton Halt (and its trademark poplars) can be seen just beyond the Elms Lane bridge in the distance. In great contrast to modern times, the A49 trunk road to the right was devoid of traffic
RUSSELL MULFORD

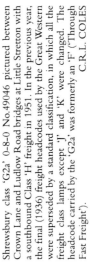

Shrewsbury class 'G2a' 0-8-0 No.49046 pictured between Crown Lane and Ludlow Road bridges at Little Stretton with a southbound Class 'H' freight in 1951. In the previous year, the final (1936) freight headcodes used by the Great Western were superseded by a standard classification, in which all the freight class lamps except 'J' and 'K' were changed. The headcode carried by the 'G2a' was formerly an 'F' ('Through Fast Freight').

C.R.L. COLES

Taking back a heavy load of 8 coaches, Swansea Paxton Street's Fowler '4MT' 2-6-4T No.42394 was approaching the Ludlow Road bridge at Little Stretton with the 3.5 p.m. Shrewsbury to Swansea train for the Central Wales line in June 1955. With the relief (2.40 p.m. Shrewsbury) running ahead on that day, there must have been a considerable demand for travel over the line.

RUSSELL MULFORD

LUDLOW ROAD BRIDGE

The southernmost road bridge in the Strettons carried the former main road (latterly B4370) south-eastwards to reconnect with the A49 trunk road. It was located just beyond the southern boundary of Little Stretton village, and presented a fine view of the line as it curved around the southern part of Ragleth Hill in company with the A49 and Quinny Brook.

The beautiful south Shropshire countryside around the Strettons is seen to advantage in this panoramic view. Canton 'Britannia' No.70028 *Royal Star* is seen on the approach to Ludlow Road bridge with the 3.5 p.m. Liverpool to Cardiff (5.28 p.m. off Shrewsbury) on a Saturday in June 1955. For the engine, this was the return working of the 11.50 a.m. Swansea service, and all of the Liverpool train was destined for Cardiff with the exception of a van or two for Penzance at the rear, detached at Pontypool Road, and forwarded by the following 3.10 p.m. Manchester. Ragleth Hill (about 1,305 ft) dominates the background

RUSSELL MULFORD

Framed in the span of the Ludlow Road overbridge, a 'Castle' is seen here heading south with the 3.10 p.m. Manchester to Plymouth service in June 1955. This train ran some fifteen minutes behind the 3.5 p.m. Liverpool and, as with that train, the engine was a scheduled Canton turn, working to Pontypool Road with this train. As it was a later service in the timetable, only the front portion worked through into the West Country, whilst the rear section was detached at Bristol.

RUSSELL MULFORD

An impressive study of the Longsight through working from Pontypool Road approaching the bridge with 'Scot' No.46160 *Queen Victoria's Rifleman* at the head of the 7.40 a.m. Penzance to Manchester in 1951. The engine still had 'British Railways' on her tender, and her nine-coach train was probably the winter timetable version with portions for Manchester and Liverpool, and a coach at the rear from Kingswear to Manchester; the summer version was at least twelve vehicles.

C.R.L. COLES

Shrewsbury Standard Class '5MT' No.73036 in grimy condition is seen here with an evening up local service to Shrewsbury, approaching the Ludlow Road bridge, Little Stretton, in June 1955. This may have been the 5.12 p.m. Hereford semi-fast, although it usually carried 'A' lamps.

RUSSELL MULFORD

Working hard on the long climb from Bromfeld. Pontypool Road 'Grange' No.6820 *Kingston Grange* still had about three-quarters-of-a-mile to run to the 650ft summit with a Class '5' (old 'D') express freight. It was about to pass under the Ludlow Road bridge at the south end of Little Stretton on the 1 in 112 gradient, on 12th June 1964.

DEREK CROSS

The stretch of more open countryside immediately to the south of Little Stretton was an excellent place for photography in the afternoon sun. Here, Chester 'Hall' No.6941 *Fillongley Hall* is pictured at the head of the 10.20 a.m. Kingswear to Manchester and Paignton to Liverpool service on a summer Saturday in June 1955. When running to time, the two portions would terminate in their respective cities a few minutes after 7.0 p.m.; no refreshment facilities were provided on the train, though it did have a 14-minute stop at Temple Meads. By this time, the excitement of the journey was probably wearing thin for some of the younger holidaymakers.

RUSSELL MULFORD

Bath Road 'Modified Hall' No.6982 *Melmerby Hall* at the head of train '244', the 8.25 a.m. Ilfracombe to Manchester, approaching Ludlow Road bridge, Little Stretton, on a summer Saturday in June 1955. This was the last in a series of seven through trains from the West Country that was due to pass the Strettons on Saturdays between around 2.0 and 5.0 p.m. It was not, however, the final service of the day; three more were due between about 7.0 and 10.0 p.m.
RUSSELL MULFORD

Shrewsbury '8F' 2-8-0 No.48307 with the 12.25 p.m. Swansea to Shrewsbury (Central Wales) train on the approach to Little Stretton in June 1955. The '8Fs' were common on Central Wales trains – mainly freight, but also with occasional passenger duties – and two dozen were shared between Coleham and Paxton Street. The train comprised the usual five vehicles, with a central Composite.
RUSSELL MULFORD

Banbury 'Hall' No.6906 *Chicheley Hall* with the 4.20 p.m. Hereford to Shrewsbury local service approaching Ludlow Road bridge on a summer Saturday in June 1955. Together with the earlier 1.15 p.m. Shrewsbury to Hereford local, this journey formed an intermediate return trip to the working of the Dorrington milk train in both directions as far as Banbury. RUSSELL MULFORD

'Royal Scot' No.46169 *The Boy Scout* was returning north off the through working to Pontypool Road with the Saturday 7.50 a.m. Newquay to Manchester (3.15 p.m. off Pontypool Road) in June 1955. This train ran a few minutes behind the 10.20 a.m. Kingswear, and took the St. Philip's Marsh route around Bristol, though unlike the Kingswear, it was provided with a dining car (an LMR vehicle, onwards from Plymouth). RUSSELL MULFORD

Approaching Marshbrook from the north, Canton 'Castle' No.5046 *Earl Cawdor* was coasting down the 1 in 112 down gradient with the 3.0 p.m. Liverpool to Cardiff (5.5 p.m. Shrewsbury) in 1951. Except on Fridays and Saturdays, this service conveyed a Manchester to Plymouth portion at the rear, detached at Pontypool Road to form the 7.25 p.m. thence. On Fridays and Saturdays. the West Country portion was much expanded to form the 3.15 p.m. Manchester to Plymouth train, which ran fifteen minutes behind the Cardiff service. The Marshbrook distant signal is seen behind the train.　　　C.R.L. COLES

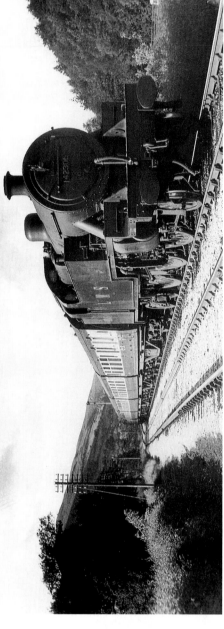

At the same location. Paxton Street's Fowler 2-6-4T No.42305 was returning to Swansea Victoria with the 5.30 p.m. from Shrewsbury in 1951. This service was scheduled for a five-coach corridor set, which started with the 7.25 a.m., Swansea to Shrewsbury, then ran an early afternoon train to Stafford and back, returning with the 5.30 p.m. pictured here.

C.R.L. COLES

MARSHBROOK

Marshbrook station stood at 15m 33ch, with its platforms to the south of the level crossing carrying the Newtown road over the main lines. To the south of the station, there was a small mileage yard on the up side, connected to the Up Main, with two dead-end sidings, together with a loading dock with cattle pen on a spur near the end of the shorter up platform.

In 1887, both platforms were extended southwards, with the up platform now also occupying the area formerly used by the cattle pens, which were moved sideways (westwards) to a position behind the new extension. At the same time, the yard was provided with a trailing connection from the Down Main.

A signal box was located to the north of the level crossing on the down side.

Passenger facilities were closed in June 1958, and goods in December 1963, the yard being removed in 1964.

Marshbrook station looking north, viewed from the Down platform in the early 1950s. The Up platform shelter is seen on the left, with the level crossing carrying the Horderley road (for Newtown) in the centre. Marshbrook signal box and station buildings are to the right. Signals of both GWR and L & NW origin are to be seen.   R.S. CARPENTER

Running past the tall Marshbrook home signal, another Paxton Street 2-6-4 tank No.42390 is seen approaching the station with the 3.5 p.m. Shrewsbury to Swansea Victoria 'express' service in the early 1950s. Carrying 'A' lamps, it took nearly four hours for the 115-mile journey to Swansea, calling at 16 of the 38 intermediate stations or halts on the Central Wales line.   C.R.L. COLES

62

Little Oakwood

M.S Ludlow — 13

376
1·836

362
·654

1·699

361
3·378

528

79
·267

82
1·261

83
2·323

363
·131

374
2·251

3·785

81
7·466

F.P.

5·835

365ª
·059

80
·119

F.P.

S.P

527 { 148
·070

Lodge

364 1·299

366ª
·025

149
·210

524

S.B

371
·692

365
·183

366
·208

Station Inn

S.B

Station

F.B.

C.S.

84
·652

2·428

367
·161

S.P

L.B

521

368
·590

C.S.

534

W.M

147
·568

539

·85 ·470

B.M.537·7

R.O

1·299

Old Quarry

150
·242

88
4·173

151
2·608

521

G.P

B.M.520·1

84ª *Agricultural*
Hall
1·083

87
3·569

89
·862

F.P.

M a r s h b r o o k

86
1·018

S.P

F.B.

Tk. O.S.

84
12·585

F.P.

92
·742

152
1·064 518

Rose Villa
(P.H)

Spring

90
1·558

F.P.

91
·885

M o

93
10·470

96
675

Heading south through Marshbrook station, the five-coach 2.45 p.m. Shrewsbury to Swansea Victoria is seen behind Paxton Street Fowler 2-6-4T No.42305 on Whit Monday, 10th June 1957. Paxton Street housed six of these tanks in 1957; they moved on to Landore in September 1959 with the closure of the ex-L & NW shed, and on to Swansea East Dock in 1961. The rear of the train was passing over the level crossing, at which a 'B' road passed across on its way to the A49, a short distance off to the right.   MICHAEL MENSING

The 12.45 p.m. Cardiff to Manchester express (11.15 Swansea) speeding through Marshbrook behind Canton 'Castle' No.5020 *Trematon Castle* in 1951. The goods yard remained in situ until April 1964, and was little used, although a van can be seen in the spur next to the up main.   C.R.L. COLES

Against a backdrop of trees to the south of the station, a northbound holiday express approaching Marshbrook behind Old Oak 'Modified Hall' No.6966 *Witchingham Hall* at around 7 p.m. on Saturday 27th July 1963. The surviving 4-6-0s were still much used on holiday traffic, although the 'Warships' based at Laira and Newton were by this time working regularly on North & West services.

MICHAEL MENSING

'Grange' No.6867 *Peterson Grange* from Pontypool Road shed heading south near Marsh Farm Jct. with a freight on 16th September 1960. At this time, Pontypool Road had eight 'Granges' to work two large diagrams, involving five of the engines daily. Apart from one day's trip to Llanelly and Margam, all their duties took them onto the North & West route, bound for Crewe, Coton Hill or Saltney.

D.B. LEWIS

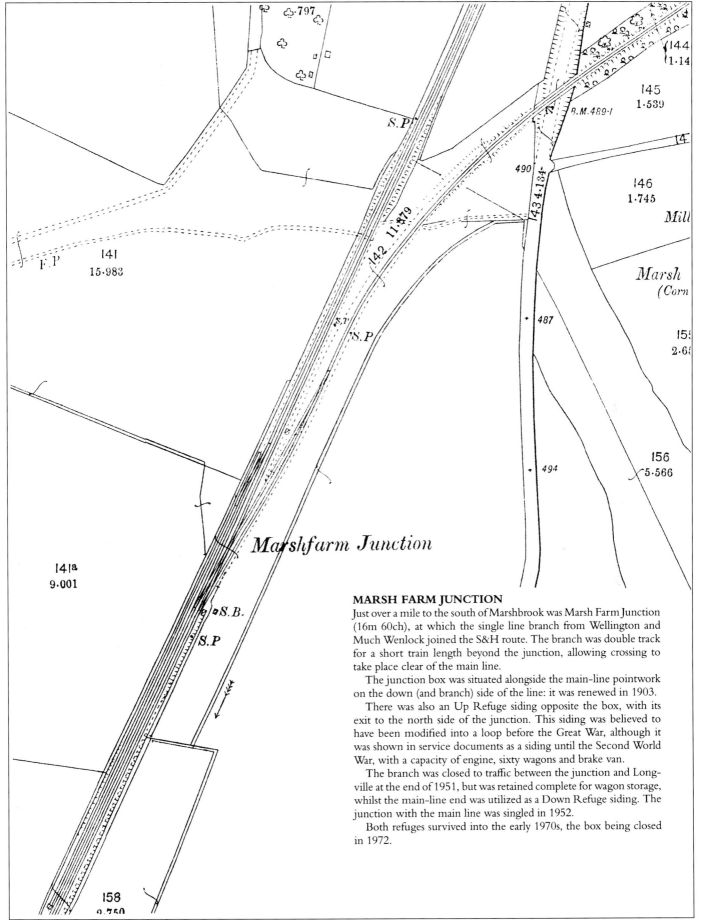

MARSH FARM JUNCTION

Just over a mile to the south of Marshbrook was Marsh Farm Junction (16m 60ch), at which the single line branch from Wellington and Much Wenlock joined the S&H route. The branch was double track for a short train length beyond the junction, allowing crossing to take place clear of the main line.

The junction box was situated alongside the main-line pointwork on the down (and branch) side of the line: it was renewed in 1903.

There was also an Up Refuge siding opposite the box, with its exit to the north side of the junction. This siding was believed to have been modified into a loop before the Great War, although it was shown in service documents as a siding until the Second World War, with a capacity of engine, sixty wagons and brake van.

The branch was closed to traffic between the junction and Longville at the end of 1951, but was retained complete for wagon storage, whilst the main-line end was utilized as a Down Refuge siding. The junction with the main line was singled in 1952.

Both refuges survived into the early 1970s, the box being closed in 1972.

WISTANSTOW HALT

Wistanstow was another of the halts opened in the area during the mid-1930s, in this instance on 7th May 1934 (at 18m 31ch). The halt was located a quarter-mile to the east of the village, and was reached from an overbridge carrying the lane from the village to the nearby A49 trunk road.

Around the turn of the century, Wistanstow was provided with a signal box (17m 74ch), some 1¼ miles from Marsh Farm box, and a similar distance from Bishop's Castle Jct. box to the south. By the Great War, the box's use had become intermittent, it was shown as disused in 1924, and closed during the winter of 1933.

Wistanstow Halt was closed in 1956.

BISHOP'S CASTLE JUNCTION

This junction (at 19m 07ch), first formed in 1866, saw the divergence of the Plowden, Lydham Heath and Bishop's Castle branch. The signal box at the junction with the main line was originally called Stretford Bridge Jct. but was renamed in 1901. The Bishop's Castle branch closed in April 1935 and the junction, box and signals were removed in 1937.

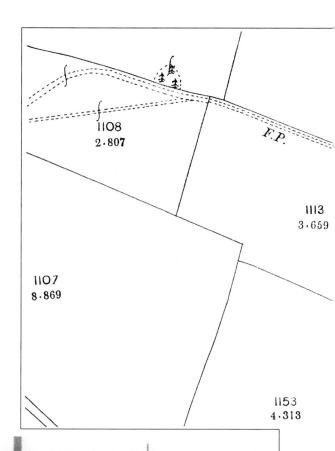

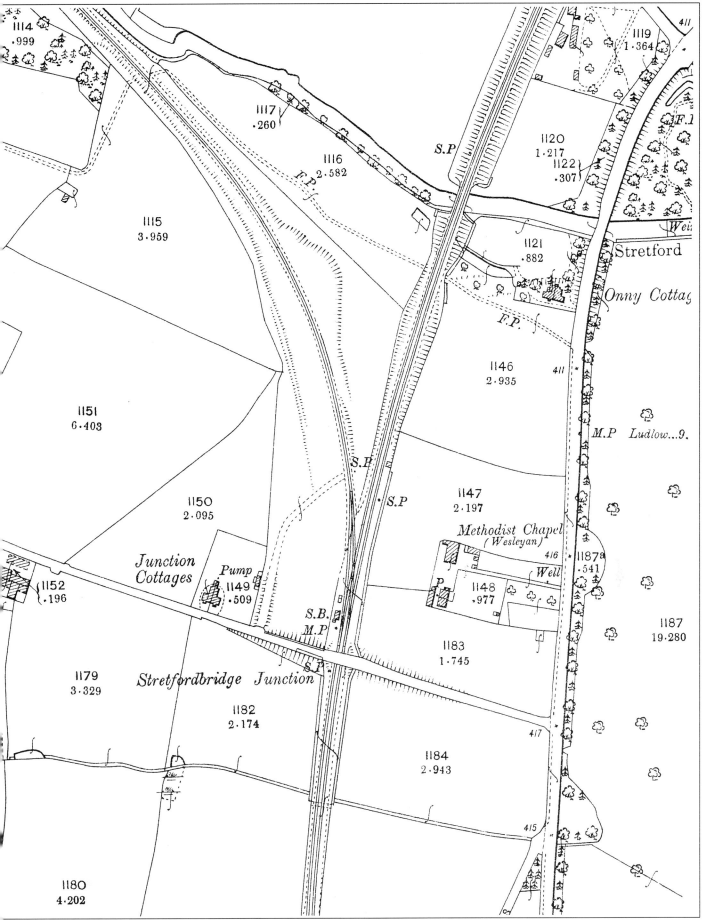

Taken from 25-inch Ordnance Survey for 1903. Crown copyright reserved.

To the north of Craven Arms, at just after 11.0 am. on Whit Monday, 10th June 1957, the 7.45 a.m. Swansea Victoria to Shrewsbury was hauled by Canton Standard Class '4MT' No.75022, probably borrowed to cover for a shortage at Paxton Street. Again, a five-coach corridor set was being used, with both carmine & cream and maroon liveries evident.

MICHAEL MENSING

CRAVEN ARMS & STOKESAY

The north end of Craven Arms station in June 1964, with Swansea East Dock Standard Class '4MT' 2-6-4T No.80069 departing with a service from the Central Wales line. The carriage shed is seen on the right, with the ex-L & NW engine shed to its left, behind the departing train. '57XX' Pannier No.4623 was shunting the goods yard, which was equipped with an overhead gantry crane.

DEREK CROSS

The station at Craven Arms (at 19m 76ch) was opened 21st April 1852, at which time it was a simple through station, though it became a junction on 6th March 1861 with the completion of the L&NW line to Knighton, the first part of that company's route to Llandovery (and Swansea). The station also handled traffic from the Bishop's Castle branch (via Stretford Bridge Jct.) from 1st February 1866, and from the Wellington and Much Wenlock line (via Marsh Farm Jct.) from 16th December 1867. Its initial title was Craven Arms, with 'Stokesay' being added in 1879.

The station had platform faces for the Down (southbound) and Up (northbound) main lines, with a bay at each end of the western face of the Up (island) platform for some originating and terminating movements. The south bay had an independent route onto the Central Wales line, avoiding the main lines. To the north, another relief line was provided alongside the Up Main with a connection from the North Bay, and this extended out as far as Long Lane Crossing, Newington, where that road passed over the railway on the level.

Craven Arms main station buildings were on the down side, directly accessible from the town and the nearby A49 trunk road. Verandahs were added to the station buildings in the late 1850s.

The other principal features of the 1870s layout were a large goods yard north of the station on the down side, with a goods shed fed by two sidings, both equipped with wagon turntables. Another three wagon turntables were provided to connect the goods loop line with two long yard sidings used for working full load traffic. Three coal businesses traded from here at the time. A further siding to the outer edge of the yard was added by 1903.

A small, single-line engine shed had been erected in 1856 by the S & HR company, to the west of the station. As traffic increased, this was found wanting, and plans for a new, four-road shed were

approved by the L&NW. The new building, constructed in local stone, was opened in 1869, with a coal stage on the east side, and coal storage sidings, water facilities and a 42ft turntable adjacent. L&NW facilities at Craven Arms were primarily for Central Wales services.

In the mid-1870s, a number of additional facilities were provided. These included a Refuge siding on the down side between Bishop's Castle Junction and Long Lane Crossing, accommodating an engine, 37 wagons and brake van. Two further up sidings were added parallel to (and to the west of) the up loop, between Long Lane Crossing and the station, one of which was designated the Up Refuge siding.

There were three signal boxes controlling the complex in the 1870s, the most northerly being on the up side at Long Lane Crossing, controlling the level crossing, the entry to the Goods Yard loop on the down side, and the Up loop into which the up bay platform line was connected. Craven Arms & Stokesay box was located at the north end of the down platform (at 19m 71ch), controlling the exit from the Goods Shed, movements in and out of the Engine Shed and the station area. South of the station (at 20m 08ch) stood Central Wales Junction box, controlling the southern approaches and the branch movements; the Central Wales line was doubled in 1872.

A train shed was also provided over the south bay, to afford protection for the Central Wales passengers at that platform.

By 1902, the goods shed was served by just the one through line, and only one wagon turntable now survived, on the shed road to its south.

In 1907, the L&NW built a capacious six-road carriage shed immediately to the north of the engine shed. The goods yard had also been extended to include a lengthy loading dock, with cattle pens. Just outside the yard was Railway Terrace, mostly accommodating railway families.

In the final months of steam, express passenger engines were to be found on virtually any duty, including lowly freight turns. Here, No.5056 *Earl of Powis* was approaching Craven Arms with a down class '9' ('K') goods train on 5th June 1964, shortly before her transfer from Hereford (86C) shed. She had still been working Royal Trains in 1959. In the distance, between the train and the goods shed, can be seen the gates and box of Craven Arms Crossing.

MILLBROOK HOUSE/DAVID JOHNSON COLLECTION

The line that ran around the back of the island platform (outside the bays) was modified to operate as a through line for goods movements, and in later times was designated 'Up & Down Goods'.

By the 1930s, the last wagon turntable in the goods yard had now disappeared, largely in line with similar alterations in goods yards all around the system, being replaced by pointwork as necessary. Two shorter sidings to the north of the goods yard had been let as private sidings to the Government Timber Supplies Department in 1919, these being taken over by South Shropshire Farmers in 1931. On the south side of the engine shed, two further short private sidings had been created and let to J.C. Edge, serving a woodworking factory, in 1922. A siding alongside was used by the Craven Arms Gas Co.

Long Lane Crossing box was replaced by a new structure on the down side in 1931, opposite the old site.

During the wartime expansion of goods facilities on the line, the Down Refuge siding was extended northwards with a connection from the Down Main, in October 1941. As with the others to its north, this now accommodated 65 wagons in addition to the engine and van; it was still shown in use in 1972.

Further signal box alterations took place in 1956. The station box was closed, and its functions were shared by Long Lane Crossing (renamed 'Craven Arms Crossing') and Central Wales Jct. (renamed Craven Arms Junction). A ground frame was provided between the goods shed and down platform for residual movements in the goods yard.

Following the withdrawal of the Much Wenlock & Wellington services in 1951, the north bay had become increasingly little used,

and with the removal of the station box (together with virtually all the pointwork at the northern end of the platforms) the bay line and its connecting road out to Craven Arms Crossing were converted into a refuge siding. The adjacent 'Up & Down Goods Loop' was specified to hold two trains.

Alterations to the layout in 1965/66 in preparation for the introduction of MAS saw the lines for up and down bay platforms taken out of use, as were the Up Refuge Siding and the Up & Down Goods Loop running behind the station. Virtually all the trackwork at the south end was removed, leaving just a trailing connection into the Up Main at the south end of the up platform for the newly-singled Central Wales line. The former junction with the Central Wales line was lifted, and Craven Arms Jct. box closed.

The engine shed was also closed in 1965, but retained for storage purposes; however, by 1971 the shed and all its facilities had disappeared.

In March 1969, all the remaining goods yard sidings were taken out of use, leaving only a short siding and a spur at the north end of the down platform, operated by the ground frame. The station buildings were demolished, and replaced by shelters.

After these alterations, the only signal box remaining was Craven Arms Crossing, the gates at which were removed in August 1969 and replaced by single lifting barriers. The former carriage shed remained in use, having been taken over by the Engineers, and remained rail connected with storage tracks for a while longer.

A view of Craven Arms station on Friday, 7th September 1951, looking south. In the bay platform to the right, a '44XX' was awaiting departure with a local service to Wellington; the train was formed with a pair of corridor coaches, providing some comfort on the 28½-mile, 100-minute journey.

R.C. RILEY/TRANSPORT TREASURY

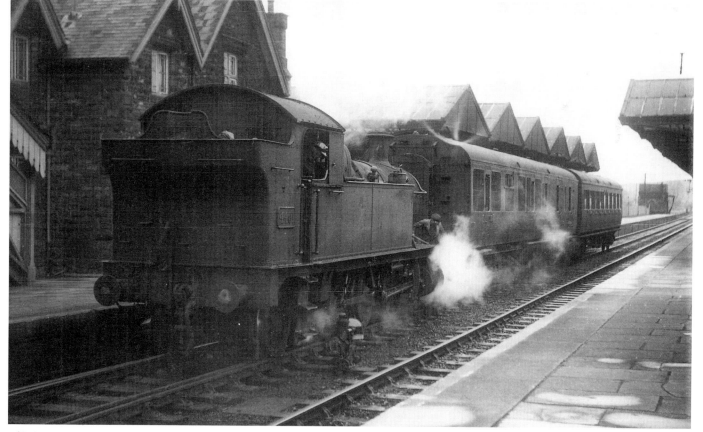

Having run round its train, Wellington shed's '4400' class 2-6-2T No.4401 is seen being recoupled to its pair of coaches at the down platform to form a return service to the Much Wenlock and Wellington line, c.1950. By this time, there were just three passenger movements daily into and out of Craven Arms over that route, and these were withdrawn at the end of 1951; the portion of the branch between Marsh Farm Jct. and Longville (some seven miles) was closed to traffic, although it was retained throughout for wagon storage until 1955, and for a short distance from the junction until 1972.

LENS OF SUTTON

F.P.

40

Lod.

46

Newington House

1256
4·064

M.P. S.P.

405

S.P.
B.

128
·108

130
·620

40 R.H.

40

Newington Villa

Smith
B.M. 402·6

Allotment Gardens
127ª
1·988

S.P.
129 ·762

131
2·938

4 ft. R.H.

Def.

4 ft. R.H.

401

Allotme
Garde

7ᵇ
1·2

5
3·737

399

391

32
1·404

W.M.

S.P.

Travelling Crane

6

274

Cattle

4
·448

Pens

12
·720

Railw
396

S.P.
S.P.
P.
P. P.

15
15·428

395

S.B.

S.P.

W.M.

L.B.

13
·469

Craven Arms & Stokesay St

S.P.

16
3·246

14
3·912

393

S.P.

F.P.

M.S.

en A r

Tank

35
·992

36
1·293

S.P.

37
1·453

390

S.P.

M.P.
34
·266

B.

4
·171

P.

33
·517

B.M.

S.P.

Craven Hotel
390

Old M.S.
Auction

38·158
Sluice

71
·861

Wales Junction
72
1·243

S.P.

S.P.

A common sight in the early 1950s: ex-L & NW Class 'G2a' 0-8-0 No.49064 of Abergavenny shed trundling south through Craven Arms station on 11th June 1951 with a mixed class 'H' goods. This was probably bound for Abergavenny, where the train would be divided into its component sections for various South Wales' yards. This engine would soon move to Tredegar shed, and become a regular performer on the summer weekend excursions to Barry Island.

R.K. BLENCOWE COLLECTION

No.4401 alongside the Down platform with an afternoon arrival from Wellington and Much Wenlock on 21st April 1951. This was probably the 3.10 p.m. Wellington service (due Craven Arms at 4.40 p.m.), the last westbound train of the day to the west of Much Wenlock, which formed the 5.0 p.m. departure for Wellington, the last eastbound train over that section of the branch. Here corridor stock featured in the formation.

W.A. CAMWELL, STEPHENSON LOCOMOTIVE SOCIETY COLLECTION

Craven Arms station, looking north on Saturday, 10th September 1949. On the up platform, the large 'Craven Arms & Stokesay' board detailed connecting stations on or via the Central Wales line, whilst the subsidiary board to its left advertised the line to Much Wenlock and Wellington, and also mentioned Market Drayton, on the Wellington to Crewe route. The up bay (south) had its own 'train shed' – an overall roof covered the line as well as the platform.　　　H.C. CASSERLEY

Shrewsbury 'Castle' No.5097 *Sarum Castle* waiting at the down platform with the 10.10 a.m. Shrewsbury to Hereford local on 10th September 1949, due to call between 11.1 and 11.4 a.m. The 'Castle' may have been running-in after a depot repair, or a substitution for a Coleham Class '5MT', which was scheduled for this turn by 1951 (and at least into the mid-1950s), returning with the 2.55 p.m. semi-fast from Hereford to Shrewsbury.　　　H.C. CASSERLEY

Paxton Street Stanier '8F' 2-8-0 No. 48665 heading through the down main line with a southbound Class 'F' goods for the Central Wales line on 10th September 1949. This was probably the 9.20 a.m. Coleham to Swansea Victoria, due through Craven Arms at 10.21 a.m.   H.C. CASSERLEY

Locally-based Webb 2-4-2T No.46727 shunting at Craven Arms. The engine was probably working as the passenger pilot, withdrawing the empty coaches from the up bay (south end) of a Central Wales train – possibly the stock of the 6.30 a.m. Swansea, to release the train engine – on 10th September 1949.
H.C. CASSERLEY

The 6.15 a.m. Swansea Victoria to Craven Arms service (due 10.8 a.m.) running into the up bay (south) behind Paxton Street's Fowler 2-6-4T No.42305 on 10th September 1949. The official formation of this train was Van Third, Compo, Van Third, and its next duty was the 2.20 p.m. to Llandovery and back, returning to Swansea the following morning as the 7.40 a.m. Craven Arms. The remainder of the passenger services at this end of the Central Wales line ran through to and from Shrewsbury at this time   H.C. CASSERLEY

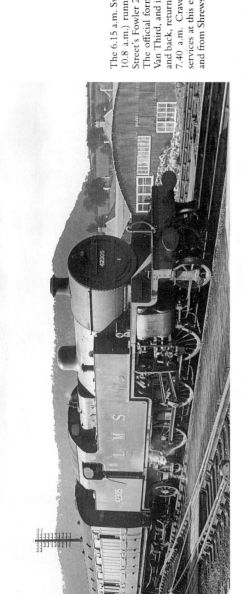

Locally-based Webb 2-4-2T No.46727 shunting at Craven Arms. The engine was probably working as the passenger pilot, withdrawing the empty coaches from the up bay (south end) of a Central Wales train – possibly the stock of the 6.30 a.m. Swansea, to release the train engine – on 10th September 1949.

H.C. CASSERLEY

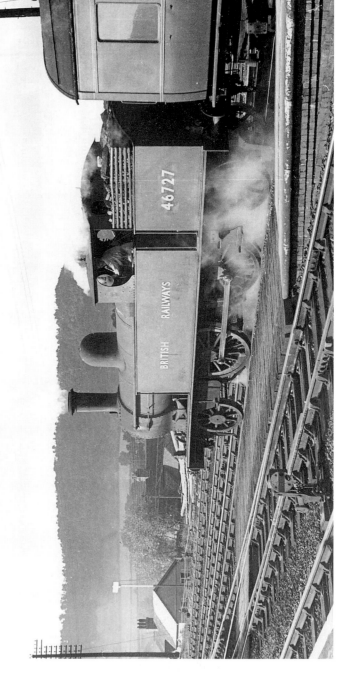

Shrewsbury 'County' No.1003 *County of Wilts* approaching Craven Arms station on the up main with the 4.20 p.m. Hereford to Shrewsbury local passenger in 1951. There was a short respite in the climb for northbound trains here, as the gradient fell towards the station for about three-quarters of a mile, although it resumed immediately beyond.
C.R.L. COLES

An unusual view of the 2.40 p.m. Shrewsbury to Swansea Victoria service double-headed by two Paxton Street Fowler 2-6-4 tanks, Nos.42385 and 42305, standing at the down platform in 1951. No.42305 was still in its final LMS livery, whilst 42385 carried lining and the early BR 'pedalling lion' emblem. The presence of two engines was probably accounted for by a previous imbalance in passenger workings, or of one of the pair returning after a failure, or perhaps some attention at Derby works.
C.R.L. COLES

A good view of the shed is afforded on 28th September 1957, showing '3F' 0-6-0s Nos. 43679 and 43822, with 'G2' 0-8-0 No.49113. The stone-built structure had a hipped roof, with ventilation over the ridges and through the roofs.
R.O. TUCK

A visit to the shed on 28th September 1957 found two former 'Earls', Nos. 9004/14, similarly in store. At the turn of that year, the surviving engines of the class (22) were 'stored', though eight emerged for the summer service in June, the remainder being condemned. Nos.9004 and 9014 both went to Croes Newydd shed, probably for duties on the Barmouth line, but were back in store on 16th September.
R.O. TUCK

Craven Arms was the type of remote depot where veteran engines would often be based, as was the case with this ex-Midland Johnson '2F' 0-6-0 No.58213, seen on 11th September 1952. Originally one of that company's '1357' class, the engine (then No.3084) was rebuilt with a Belpaire boiler in 1919. and is seen here with a tender cab, which would no doubt have proved to be of great benefit on winter trips over the Central Wales route. However, she was also used on station pilot duties.
H.C. CASSERLEY

A view outwards from the shed doors on 28th September 1957, showing ex-Midland '3F' No 43679 from Shrewsbury (or sub-shedded here) and ex-North Western 'G2' class 0-8-0 No.49113 from Pontypool Road. The allocation of banking engines at the shed to assist over the gradients towards Knighton was by now largely a memory.
R.O. TUCK

A view of the south end of Craven Arms shed on 2nd June 1964, with '8F' No.48400 and 57XX' No.4623 on view. The shed had only three of the original four roads still in situ, the far line having been removed in 1937. Beyond the stone-built office can be seen the coal stage, turntable (beyond the '57XX') and water crane. B.J. ASHWORTH

With plenty of accommodation, and only a few engines allocated, Craven Arms shed was a useful place to hold engines in store, particularly from Coleham. Here, Johnson '2F' 0-6-0 No.58207 and Webb 'Coal Tank' 0-6-2T No. 58904 (both formerly of Coleham) were both in store on 20th July 1955, with the usual sacking over the chimney. The '2F' would be sent to Crewe/Derby in the following month for condemnation, as would the 'Coal Tank' to Crewe. R.O. TUCK

Craven Arms station, looking northwards c.1950. This view shows all of the major facilities at the site with the exception of Central Wales Junction, which was just off the bottom of the picture.
AERO PICTORIAL LTD.

An ailing Newton Abbot 'Warship' diesel No.D838, assisted by Hereford 'Castle' No.5000 *Launceston Castle* – herself looking the worse for wear – working the 8.0 a.m. Plymouth to Liverpool on Friday, 5th June 1964. No.5000 would probably have been acting as the Hereford up line pilot for such eventualities, probably one of the last duties; she left Hereford later in the month, but No.5056 stayed until November of that year. Central Wales Junction box can be seen to the right.
DEREK CROSS

Passing through the station on 5th June 1964, Crewe North's 'Britannia' 4-6-2 No.70025 *Western Star* is pictured with a very lengthy class 'C' Heysham to Weymouth Pigeon Special. At one time, the railways carried a very significant amount of racing pigeon traffic from the North of England to numerous destinations in the south, at which points they were released, usually by station staff. The engine was a familiar sight on the North & West, having been at Canton shed between April 1953 and September 1961.
DEREK CROSS

Six months after her last Heavy Intermediate at Swindon, Coleham 'Manor' No.7812 *Earlestoke Manor* was heading a short class '8' ('H') freight bound for Hereford or beyond through Craven Arms in June 1964. She was amongst the last 'Manors' to be withdrawn, in November 1965.

DEREK CROSS

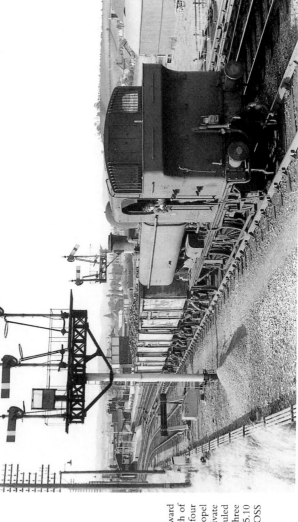

In June 1964, '57XX' 0-6-0PT No.4623 had drawn forward along the Central Wales branch 'Third Line' to the south of the station bay, and was standing near the signal box with four wagons of coal. From here, it could have been about to propel its load into the mileage yard, or into the Gas Board's private siding, or even into the engine shed sidings. The scheduled duty for the engine in the early 1960s was for some three hours shunting from 7.20 a.m., and another period from 5.10 p.m. until 8.30 p.m.

DEREK CROSS

Shrewsbury '8F' No.48409 with a class '8' train of unfitted empty mineral wagons bound for South Wales running through the station and approaching Central Wales Jct. in June 1964. The engine was built at Swindon in September 1943, and survived until March 1965. Shrewsbury shed had a few turns into the Principality at this time, mainly to Pontardulais and Llandilo Jct. via the Central Wales route, but one or two to Pontypool Road or Cardiff via the main line. A train of empty steel wagons on the move was one of the noisiest to be experienced on the railways.

DEREK CROSS

A southbound partly-fitted express train of vans running at Class '6' ('E') heading through the station in June 1964 behind Stanier '8F' No.48461. This engine was allocated to Llanelly, though the train may have been signalled for the North & West route.

DEREK CROSS

A view from a 5MT-hauled Central Wales train easing onto the up main line and passing Central Wales Jct. box on its way to the call at the station. The line on the left of the train, officially termed the 'Third Line' in documents, enabled Central Wales branch trains to run into and out of Craven Arms station up bay (south) independently of the main line. It also ran behind the station and along to Long Lane level crossing at the north end of Craven Arms, again being operative in both up and down directions.

P.J. GARLAND

This view from the signal box shows a lengthy class '8' ('H') freight coming off the Central Wales line behind Shrewsbury '8F' No.48761 in June 1964. The mixed nature of the traffic affords some idea of the variety of traffic involved on this long route into Wales, with mineral, industrial and general merchandise conveyed.

DEREK CROSS

A close-up view of the Central Wales Junction taken from a down main line train in July 1953, showing the point leading to the additional, independent 'Third Line' into Craven Arms on the right. The sharpness of the curve may be judged in this view, in particular that of the 'Third Line'. The branch was double for the first $12\frac{1}{2}$ miles to Knighton, and for shorter sections beyond that.   R.O. TUCK

This view taken from the Class '5MT'-hauled Central Wales train was taken immediately before the one featured on page 85. It shows the train approaching the junction with the North & West line and about to pass a 'Cross Country' DMU on a down stopping service on 26th June 1964. There was a 10 mph restriction over the sharp curve on the branch leading onto the main line. with additional check rails provided.   P.J. GARLAND

STOKESAY

There was a level crossing at Stokesay (20m 69ch), just to the south-west of the village, and another just beyond, at Stokeswood (21m 10ch), both operated by ground frames. These were occupation and lane crossings, removed in June 1958 and December 1963 respectively.

Against a backdrop of Stokesay Castle, one of the later series of '28XX' class 2-8-0s is seen here heading south with a Down goods on 16th September 1960. The train probably comprised empty tinplate wagons returning to South Wales.
D.B. LEWIS

Craven Arms station originally carried only the name of the nearby village, but in 1879 was renamed Craven Arms & Stokesay, the latter being a short distance to the south. The 13th century Stokesay Castle, latterly owned by the Earls of Craven, stands on the right of this picture. which shows the 11.55 a.m. Manchester to Plymouth, hauled by Canton 'Castle' No.5005 *Manorbier Castle* running through its own black exhaust in August 1953, without the usual Canton shine.
COLLECTION G.W. SHARPE

Stafford Road 'Star' No. 4053 *Princess Alexandra* leaving Onibury with a three-coach Hereford to Shrewsbury local passenger, conveying a horsebox on the rear, during 1951. Stafford Road engines were not often diagrammed between Shrewsbury and Hereford at this time, so No.4053 may have been 'borrowed' by Coleham for a return trip to Hereford before continuing her normal turn. The engine still had three years of service ahead of her, being condemned in July 1954.

C.R.L. COLES

St. Philip's Marsh 'Grange' No.6845 *Paviland Grange* passing Onibury signal box and approaching the A49 level crossing with the 2.30 p.m. Crewe to Pontypool Road parcels, c.1954. This train ran on Saturdays with regular vehicles from Stranraer, Greenock, Glasgow and Crewe destined for South Wales and the West Country, but on other days to Hereford only when the traffic justified (a minimum of ten vehicles).

ONIBURY

Onibury station (22m 72ch) was located three miles to the south of Craven Arms, at the point where the A49 trunk road crossed over the railway on the level. The trunk road traversed the line at an angle, which determined the slight offsetting of the platforms to its south. A small yard was located behind the down platform, initially consisting of one siding that curved round to run alongside the down main line, with trailing connections to the up and down running lines.

A signal box was positioned just to the north of the crossing, on the down side.

The platforms were lengthened and the connections modified in 1872, and a second siding added off the first in the yard around the turn of the century. An Up Refuge Siding was added alongside the main line in 1897, accommodating an engine, 49 wagons and brake van.

In 1954, the trailing connection from the yard to the Up Main was removed, with a separate crossover provided between the Down and Up Mains.

Passenger and freight facilities were both withdrawn on 9th June 1958, though the down sidings and connections with and between the main lines were not taken out of use until March 1961. The Up Refuge Siding followed in April 1964.

The original signal box on the down side was closed at the end of 1977, replaced by a new installation on the up side to the south of the crossing, which was now protected by barriers.

Onibury, facing north, showing the cluster of structures around the level crossing, with the main station building on the right, and the signal box beyond, seen on 14th July 1963, some five years after the removal of passenger facilities. The platforms were to the near side of the gates, but had been removed by this time.
H.C. CASSERLEY

Onibury station house and part of the level crossing, after closure, looking north towards Craven Arms.
COLLECTION R.K. BLENCOWE

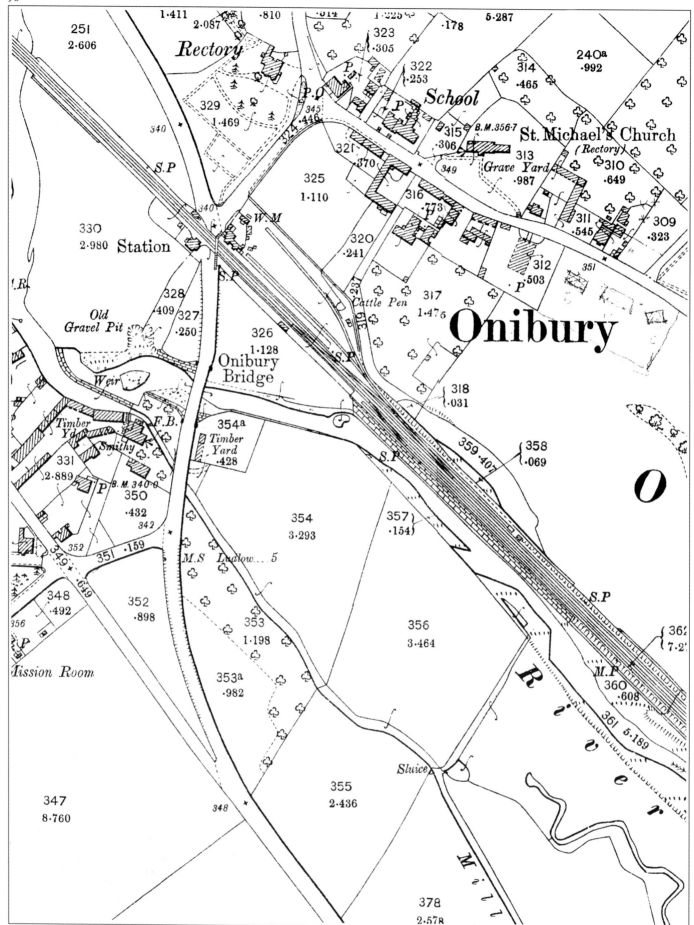

On the easy run through Onibury where, in the up direction, the gradient steepens only from 1 in 420 to 286. Canton 'Castle' No.5030 *Shirburn Castle* is seen passing the station with the 12.45 p.m. Cardiff to Manchester (11.15 Swansea) service. The clerestory coach positioned at the head of the train was an uncommon sight in fast traffic by this time, 1951. The up refuge siding can be seen to the right of the train, and the rather neglected goods yard to the left.   C.R.L. COLES

Other than a few heads out of windows in the leading coaches, there is little to indicate that Shrewsbury 'Castle' No.5050 *Earl of St. Germans* had just failed in the platform at Onibury on the returning double-home working from Newton Abbot with the 8.0 a.m. Plymouth to Manchester train on Saturday, 28th September 1957. After a while – and perhaps with a more plentiful supply of steam with which to face the gradients ahead – the crew managed to coax the engine forward again on to Shrewsbury, but were probably regretting they did not take advantage of the Hereford pilot.   R.O. TUCK

Following eighteen minutes behind the Liverpool to Plymouth service was the 9.10 a.m. Manchester to Cardiff and Swansea. This involved a through Longsight working to Pontypool Road, with 'Jubilee' No.45723 *Fearless* on the duty here, conveying largely WR stock on 12th June 1957. A Brake Compo from Birkenhead to Cardiff was normally attached to the rear, behind an LMR Brake Van.

R.O.TUCK

Drifting down the gentle bank from Onibury, the outward working of the double-home turn to Newton Abbot is pictured with Coleham 'Castle' No.5097 *Sarum Castle* on Wednesday, 12th June 1957. The train was the 9.10 a.m. Liverpool to Plymouth, with which the 'Castle' faced a 6½-hour journey as far as Newton. This service conveyed a dining car, and as the time would be around noon, the staff would doubtless have been busy with the first serving of lunch. Three coaches from Manchester to Paignton were positioned behind the main Plymouth portion (with an additional. strengthening coach at the head on this occasion).

R.O.TUCK

BROMFIELD

After the doubling of the line, Bromfield station (at 25m 24ch) had offset platforms to each side of a level crossing, with the down platform to the north, and the up to the south. The road crossing over the railway was a small lane running north-eastwards out of the village, which was some half-mile from the station. A signal box was located at the south end of the down platform, against the crossing. A small goods yard with a loading dock for horse traffic was provided on the up side, opposite the down platform, with trailing connections to each running line.

In 1904, the down platform was moved south of the crossing, opposite the up, and its former location was utilised for a Down Refuge Siding, on which another horse loading dock (for the adjacent Ludlow Racecourse) was situated, though curiously not on the

spur at its southern end. The siding had a capacity of 44 wagons in addition to engine and van.

The Down Refuge Siding was extended northwards and linked into the down main line in 1941 to become a Down Goods Loop, with an increased capacity of 65 wagons, the standard for the conversions on the line.

Bromfield was closed for passenger traffic on 9th June 1958. Goods facilities were withdrawn on 15th June 1964, after which the sidings and connections were taken out of use.

The signal box had received a new frame in April 1956, and the crossing was protected by new barriers from November 1975. Along with the box, the down goods loop remained under MAS beyond the age of steam.

A view of Bromfield, looking south, showing the goods yard on the north side of the level crossing on 14th July 1963. The Down Goods Loop, nearest the camera, was extended from the original Down Refuge Siding in 1941, increasing the capacity from 44 to 65 wagons (in addition to engine & brake van). The small goods yard to the right contained one long siding with spurs off the ends; goods services continued until June 1964. The home signals are on the bracket, with a ground signal on the right.   H.C. CASSERLEY

Bromfield station building, level crossing and footbridge on 14th July 1963, looking very similar to its neighbour at Onibury. The building on the right was the original station, with platform attached, though in later times two much longer platforms were positioned on the far side (to the south-east) of the gates. The station underwent a number of alterations to the platform arrangement between the doubling of c.1861 and provision of the Down Refuge Siding (with the associated platform move) around 1904. It eventually closed to passenger traffic in June 1958.   R.M. CASSERLEY

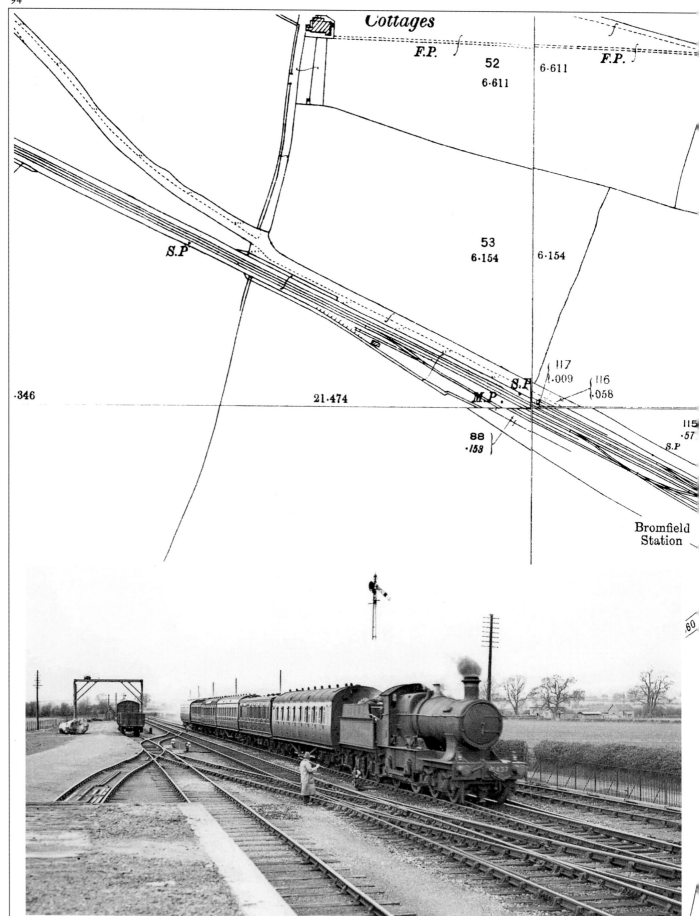

Cottages

F.P.

52
6·611

6·611

F.P.

53
6·154

6·154

S.P

·346

21·474

117
·009

116
·058

S.P

M.P.

88
·153

115
·57
S.P

Bromfield
Station

60

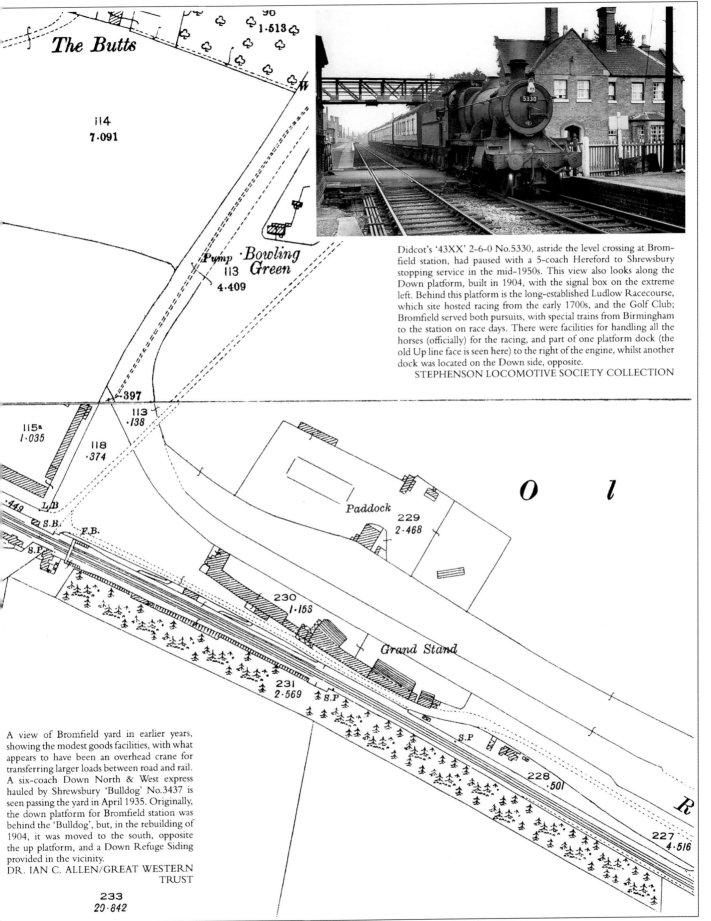

The Butts

114
7·091

90
1·513

Pump ·*Bowling*
113 *Green*
4·409

·397

113
·138

115ª
1·035

118
·374

·449

L.B

S.B.

F.B.

S.P.

Paddock
229
2·468

230
1·153

Grand Stand

231
2·569
S.P

S.P

228
·501

227
4·516

O   l

R

233
20·842

Didcot's '43XX' 2-6-0 No.5330, astride the level crossing at Bromfield station, had paused with a 5-coach Hereford to Shrewsbury stopping service in the mid-1950s. This view also looks along the Down platform, built in 1904, with the signal box on the extreme left. Behind this platform is the long-established Ludlow Racecourse, which site hosted racing from the early 1700s, and the Golf Club; Bromfield served both pursuits, with special trains from Birmingham to the station on race days. There were facilities for handling all the horses (officially) for the racing, and part of one platform dock (the old Up line face is seen here) to the right of the engine, whilst another dock was located on the Down side, opposite.
STEPHENSON LOCOMOTIVE SOCIETY COLLECTION

A view of Bromfield yard in earlier years, showing the modest goods facilities, with what appears to have been an overhead crane for transferring larger loads between road and rail. A six-coach Down North & West express hauled by Shrewsbury 'Bulldog' No.3437 is seen passing the yard in April 1935. Originally, the down platform for Bromfield station was behind the 'Bulldog', but, in the rebuilding of 1904, it was moved to the south, opposite the up platform, and a Down Refuge Siding provided in the vicinity.
DR. IAN C. ALLEN/GREAT WESTERN TRUST

Taken from 25-inch Ordnance Survey for 1926. Crown copyright reserved.

An unidentified 'Hall' approaching the Felton Farm overbridge, beyond the troughs, with the 10.20 a.m. Kingswear to Crewe service on Saturday, 1st September 1956. This was a 'block reservation' train, as were a number on busy days from Torbay, and required a (free) reservation to travel, the ticket being stamped with the number of the train (588 in this instance). Through coaches to Manchester and Liverpool were provided. The engine for this train was scheduled for an Exeter 'Hall' to Pontypool Road, and a Pontypool Road 'Grange' to Shrewsbury.
RUSSELL MULFORD

Longsight 'Patriot' No.45520 *Llandudno* heading north over the troughs with what was probably the 7.50 a.m. Newquay to Manchester, which the engine would have taken over at Pontypool Road, on Saturday, 1st September 1956. On weekdays, the engine worked the 7.30 a.m. Penzance to Manchester, again from Pontypool Road. The leading pair of coaches (including a dining car) ran from Plymouth, whilst the remainder worked from Newquay, all destined for London Road station.
RUSSELL MULFORD

LUDLOW TROUGHS

In 1895, the Great Western opened the first of its water troughs on the main lines at Goring, and during the following eleven years increased the provision to 14 locations throughout the system. The second set of troughs to be opened was at Ludlow, for which authority had been given even before the Goring set. Opened on 23rd April 1896, seven months after Goring, the troughs were located one mile to the north of Ludlow station on a three-quarters-of-a-mile level section of trackbed alongside the A49 trunk road; they were 1,838 feet in length, with a trough to each line, built at a total cost of £3,860.

With non-stop running of express passenger services between Shrewsbury and Hereford, the troughs were well positioned at the halfway point of the journey (26 miles), and also permitted a similar convenience to the express freight services of later years that also did not call intermediately.

The troughs were academic to this afternoon, one-trailer railmotor service, the 3.15 p.m. Leominster to Craven Arms and the 4.5 p.m. return to Tenbury Wells, seen on Friday, 9th May 1958. The outbound trip, with Hereford/Leominster 0-4-2T No.1456 leading, is seen against the distant backdrop of Ludlow, whilst the return trip highlights the five-compartment trailer No. W248W, rebuilt from Brake Third No.4016 in June 1955. This auto worked a morning sequence from Leominster over the Woofferton & Tenbury line, and in the afternoon ran from Leominster to Craven Arms and return, a couple more trips to Tenbury, and finally the 5.53 p.m. Woofferton workmen's to Craven Arms, and back to Leominster.
R.O. TUCK

A mile to the north of Ludlow station, Canton's prize possession – 'Castle' No.5020 *Trematon Castle* – is pictured on Ludlow Troughs with the 11.55 a.m. Manchester (London Rd.) to Plymouth service on Monday, 4th June 1956. The whole train (scheduled for 9 coaches in this last week of winter services), including the dining car, ran through between the two cities. On CDF Turn 12, the engine worked through from Shrewsbury (departing 2.24 p.m.) to Bristol, then home with the 8.0 p.m. passenger from Temple Meads. The slight dip under the occupation overbridge after the descent from Bromfield is evident in this view.
R.O. TUCK

During the days of mass 'Britannia' presence at Canton, when the entire fifteen of the WR fleet was concentrated there, No.70015 *Apollo* is seen on the 11.55 a.m. Manchester to Plymouth train, on Friday, 9th May 1958. She was taking up water from the 561-yard Ludlow troughs, and should have picked up the 1,200 gallons (or so) used since Shrewsbury. Nos.70015, 70017 *Arrow* and 70021 *Morning Star* were transferred from Canton to the London Midland sheds at Trafford Park and Cricklewood to work the Manchester & St. Pancras services for the summer service from July 1958.
R.O. TUCK

LUDLOW

The 9.15 a.m. Manchester to Swansea sweeping through Ludlow behind Longsight 'Royal Scot' No.46153 *The Royal Dragoon*, on her way to an engine change at Pontypool Road. A northbound goods can be seen on the up line passing the Goods Shed on the west side of the line. On the down side of the line, the yard sidings (with overhead crane, originally for timber), and the former engine shed are visible.
BRIAN MORRISON

Ludlow is the first town of any size on the S&H route out of Shrewsbury, with the station (at 27m 43ch) within its eastern part. It was the junction for the busy Clee Hill mineral branch, which joined the main line a quarter-mile to the north of the station. On the east side of the curving branch line, three storage sidings, known as Fishmore Sidings, had been provided by 1903, increased to five by 1910.

To the south of the junction, a small engine shed was located on the east side of the running lines, providing power for both the branch and for local main-line traffic, with three down traffic sidings. On the west side was the goods yard, with a shed storage line alongside the Up Main, then a goods shed with a single road running through. Three further yard mileage sidings for full load traffic were to the west of the shed, equipped with cattle pens, and connecting wagon turntables across the south end of the yard.

The station had two platforms, with the substantial main buildings on the up (west) side. Beyond was the 132-yard Ludlow tunnel.

Two refuge sidings were provided near the junction in the early years of the century. The Up Refuge ran alongside the Up Main opposite the branch, and with a designated capacity of 70 wagons may also have extended back into the yard, whilst the Down Refuge curved around the outside of the branch curve, with a capacity of 58 wagons.

There were two signal boxes at Ludlow: Clee Hill Jct., on the down side just to the south of the junction, and Ludlow Station, on the northern end of the up platform. The junction and station boxes were both closed in 1935, being replaced by a larger, centralized 'Ludlow' box just to the south of the site of the former.

The Cambrian Wagon Co. took a private siding in the downside yard by 1923; otherwise, Ludlow showed remarkably little change in its layout until after the closure of the engine shed in December 1951.

Surviving wagon turntables were removed from the south end of the goods yard during 1952/3, together with the trailing connection at that end into the Down Main, leaving the yard connected directly only with the Up Main.

The Clee Hill branch was closed at the end of 1962 although some of the branch trackwork remained, whilst the former branch running line was designated a refuge siding from 1966, taking over that function from the former siding nearby.

Goods services were withdrawn on 6th May 1968, and the yard trackwork probably did not long survive. With the introduction of MAS, Ludlow box closed in June 1968, the Up Refuge siding having been taken out the previous year.

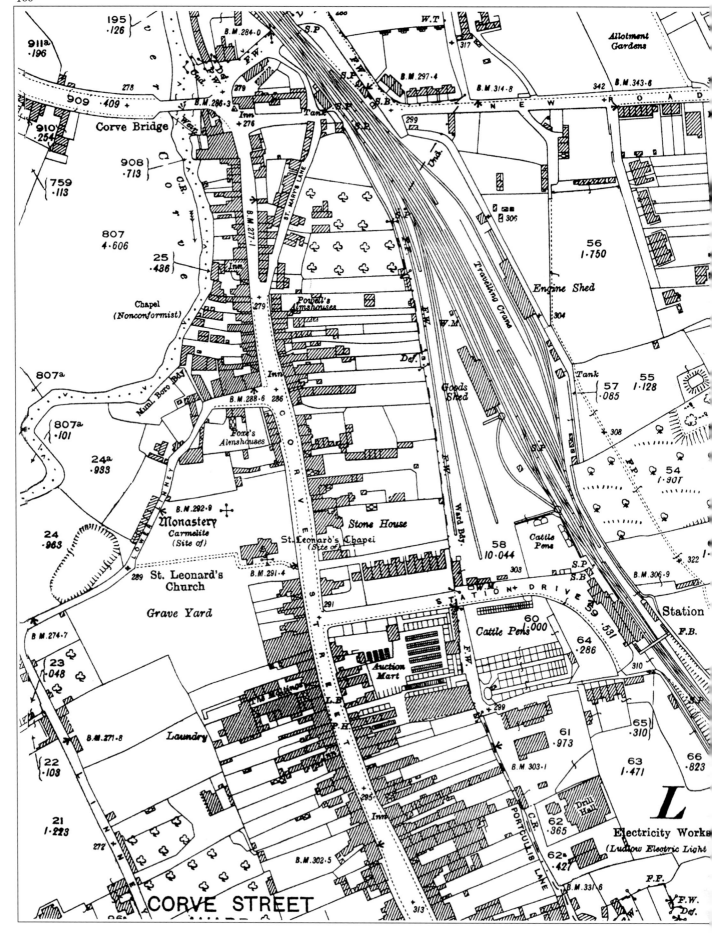

195 ·126
911ᵃ ·196
B.M.284·0
S.P
W.T
Allotment Gardens
909 ·409
910 ·254
Corve Bridge
B.M.286·3
317
B.M.297·4
299
B.M.314·8
342
B.M.343·6
N E W   R O A D
908 ·713
759 ·113
807 4·606
25 ·436
Chapel (Nonconformist)
Inn
Powell's Almshouses
56 1·750
Engine Shed
Travelling Crane
807ᵃ
807ᵃ ·101
24ᵃ ·933
Foxe's Almshouses
Goods Shed
Def.
Tank
57 ·085
55 1·128
·304
·308
54 1·90T
B.M.292·9
Monastery Carmelite (Site of)
24 ·963
St. Leonard's Chapel (Site of)
Stone House
58 10·044
Cattle Pens
S.P S.B
B.M.306·9
322
B.M.291·4
289   St. Leonard's Church
Grave Yard
303
Ward Bdy.
S T A T I O N   D R I V E
59 ·531
Station
F.B.
B.M.274·7
23 ·048
60 000
Cattle Pens
64 ·286
310
65 ·310
Laundry
B.M.271·8
61 ·973
66 ·823
22 ·103
63 1·471
B.M.303·1
62 ·365
L
21 1·223
272
Electricity Works (Ludlow Electric Light
Drill Hall
62 ·427
B.M.302·5
B.M.331·6
P.F.
F.W. Def.
313
CORVE STREET

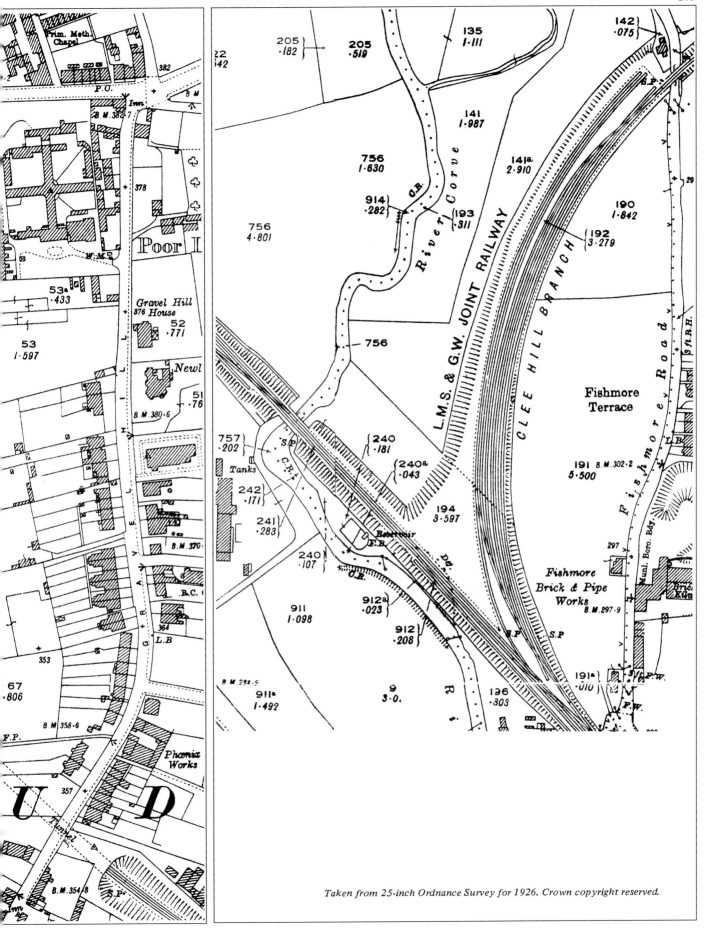

Taken from 25-inch Ordnance Survey for 1926. Crown copyright reserved.

Ludlow station, facing north on 6th August 1963, showing the goods shed in the middle distance on the left (up side), and the former engine shed to the right (down side), partially hidden behind the large bush. In the distance, Ludlow signal box can just be seen, located to the south of the junction with the Clee Hill branch which had been closed in December 1962. Originally, Ludlow Station box had been located at the north end of the up platform, but in 1935 its function was amalgamated with Clee Hill Jct. box, which was then rebuilt and renamed Ludlow box. The engine shed, which housed locomotives for the local services, was closed in 1951; in the mid-war years, when records of allocation ceased, the shed housed a '45XX' for a passenger turn and a '57XX' for goods.
J.H. MOSS

The forecourt of Ludlow station, as seen from Station Drive on 6th August 1963. The substantial buildings housed the usual passenger, parcels and staff facilities.
J.H. MOSS

Left: Ludlow station, seen from the down platform looking south towards the tunnel mouth with the up platform buildings, canopy and the footbridge evident.
Right: A study of the platform elevation of the main station buildings on the same occasion.
J.H. MOSS

The down platform waiting shelter and toilets. The footbridge had substantial brick-built stairway sections, with a lattice span.
J.H. MOSS

A panoramic view of Ludlow station and goods, seen from the embankment at the south end with Shrewsbury 'Castle' No.5038 *Morlais Castle* running through the station towards the tunnel with the 9.5 a.m. Liverpool to Plymouth service. The engine had been transferred from Old Oak Common to Shrewsbury in March 1958 following a Heavy Casual repair at Swindon, during which she appears to have been re-painted. No.5038 would remain at Shrewsbury until May 1962, when she was transferred to Oxford. In 1956, the 9.5 a.m. Liverpool was worked through to Newton Abbot by the Coleham engine, returning the next day with the 8.0 a.m. Plymouth, but from 1959, with dieselisation in the West Country, the duty ran through only to Bristol, returning from Temple Meads with the 12.0 noon Penzance.

BRIAN MORRISON

The 3.50 p.m. Leominster to Ludlow auto train (due 4.9 p.m.) emerging from the tunnel into the up platform on 14th April 1961 behind Hereford/Leominster 0-4-2T No.1445.

R.O. TUCK

Coleham 'Hall' No.5958 *Knolton Hall* emerging from the tunnel with a northbound class 'K' goods, possibly the 9.15 a.m. Hereford (Barrs Court) to Coton Hill which would doubtless have called at Ludlow Goods, on Friday, 15th August 1958.
BRIAN MORRISON

Having crossed over, the return 4.15 p.m. Ludlow to Woofferton and Tenbury Wells is seen at the down platform. The auto service between Woofferton and Tenbury was withdrawn in July 1961, along with the connecting main line auto movements.
R.O. TUCK

ASHFORD BOWDLER

On the northern approach to Ashford Bowdler, former L & NW 0–8–0 No.48945 is seen heading south through with a class 'H' goods service in 1951. The engine was from Coleham shed, and was probably hauling an Abergavenny Jct. train, possibly the 10.25 a.m. from Coleham.

C.R.L. COLES

ASHFORD CROSSING

About three miles south of Ludlow station. the railway passed through the village of Ashford Bowdler, which had a crossing controlled from a signal box (Ashford Crossing – 30m 49ch) until 1933, then by a ground frame. The road was quiet, with traffic only passing between the two parts of the village.

Canton 'Mogul' No.6352 passing Ashford Bowdler with the 6.48 a.m. Cardiff to Shrewsbury local passenger train in 1951. This was scheduled for a four-coach corridor set, with a Third and Composite between two outer Van Thirds. Two years later, an LMR engine was rostered with this train from Hereford to Shrewsbury; it may also have been the case here, though unavailability may have required the '43XX' to remain with its train.   C.R.L. COLES

Showing the variety of freight power on view, Coleham 'G2' class 0-8-0 No.49138 was headings past Ashford Bowdler with another up Class 'H' goods in 1951. The contrast between flat-bottom rail on the down main and bullhead on the up is shown here.
                                                                    C.R.L. COLES

Severn Tunnel '28XX' 2-8-0 No.2829 working hard with an early northbound goods through Ashford Bowdler in 1951. This may have been the 3.20 a.m. Pontypool Road to Saltney train, with a mixed load of mineral and merchandise (in sheeted 'Opens').
C.R.L. COLES

Poundng along through Ashford Bowdler, WD 2-8-0 No.90579 seems to have been running well, with no signs of steam leakage, at the head of a class 'H' goods in 1951. The load appears to have been coal, possibly the 2.30 a.m. Cardiff to Saltney service. No.90579 was from Banbury, and was a long way from her more familiar routes, although it was not unknown for a Banbury diagram to include a cross-country journey between the out and back legs.
C.R.L. COLES

Bath Road 'Castle' No. 7034 *Ince Castle* heading north through Ashford Bowdler in 1951 with what may have been the 10.5 a.m. Penzance to Liverpool, pictured before the train numbering system commenced that summer. The train was formed with a passenger brake and a couple of other vans at the head of the passenger accommodation.

C.R.L. COLES

Ebbw Jct 2-8-0 No.2896 running through Ashford Bowdler with a late afternoon northbound Class 'H' goods in 1951. The train could have been the 1.25 p.m. Alexandra Dock Jct. to Saltney, which was scheduled to call at Craven Arms to pick up livestock for the fast evening up freights from Shrewsbury; two cattle vehicles may already be seen at the head of the train.

C.R.L. COLES

Pontypool Road '28XX' No.2893 with an up class 'H' goods passing the goods refuge loops to the north of Woofferton Jct. in 1951, probably bound for Saltney. Originally, there was only a down refuge siding here, but in 1941 it was converted into a loop, and an up loop added, each with a capacity of 65 wagons, engine and brake van. Very many conversions and additions of this form were carried out during the war years to accommodate the massive increase in the flow of goods traffic.
C.R.L. COLES

The north end of Woofferton Jct., seen from the station footbridge on 2nd July 1949, showing the branch junction on the main line, and beyond, the line running across from the bay platform, the usual departure point for originating branch services. Woofferton Jct. signal box is seen behind the junctions, against the overbridge carrying an occupation track over the main lines. The goods shed road and cattle pens are visible to the right. Just out of sight along the branch was Woofferton engine shed, closed around the turn of the century, but still standing at this time.
COLLECTION R.S. CARPENTER

WOOFFERTON JCT.

Woofferton (at 32m 11ch) was the junction with the branch from Kidderminster, Bewdley and Tenbury Wells, 4½ miles to the south of Ludlow. Positioned just to the north of a road bridge (later the B4362), the station originally comprised two small platforms, which, after the arrival of the line from Tenbury in August 1861, were also used for the branch traffic. By 1879, the down platform had been almost doubled in length to the south.

There was a small goods yard to the north of the station on the down side, with a goods shed and the usual cattle pens and wagon turntable, the yard being connected to both the main line and the branch. A mileage siding was soon added, and connected to the branch.

Woofferton Junction box was situated within the fork between the main line and the branch; it was opened in 1875 and renewed in 1889. A small engine shed on the branch, complete with turntable, was closed by 1900.

Running north from a connection with the main line near the junction, a ballast pit siding was opened in 1876 but again had gone

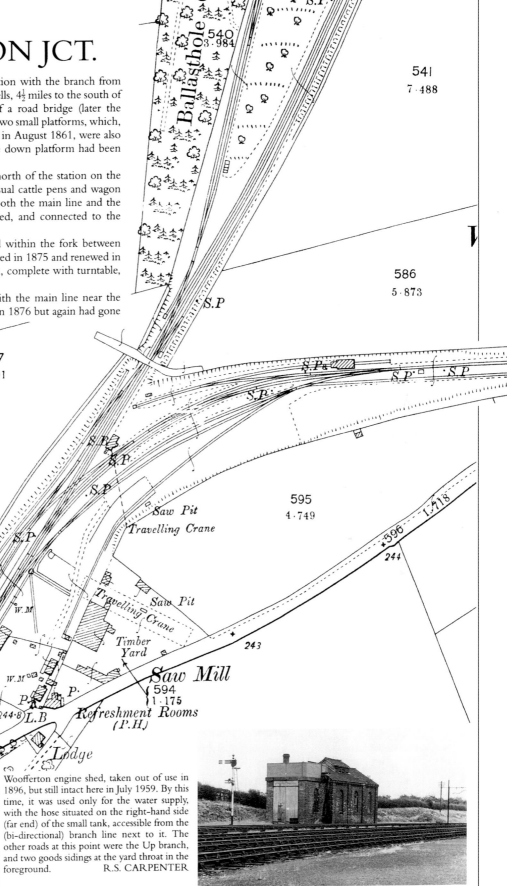

Woofferton engine shed, taken out of use in 1896, but still intact here in July 1959. By this time, it was used only for the water supply, with the hose situated on the right-hand side (far end) of the small tank, accessible from the (bi-directional) branch line next to it. The other roads at this point were the Up branch, and two goods sidings at the yard throat in the foreground.
R.S. CARPENTER

Taken from 25-inch Ordnance Survey for 1903. Crown copyright reserved.

Tenbury Wells junction after the branch platform and sidings had been removed in 1957, leaving a refuge line connecting into the Up Main only; this was eventually removed in 1964. To the right may be seen the goods yard sidings, with the cattle pens. On the far side of the branch, at the extreme right-hand edge of the picture, may be seen the end of the old engine shed, closed in the mid-1890s but retained until sometime around the closure of the branch.   J.H. MOSS

Looking south along the bay platform, showing a Tenbury Wells, Bewdley and Kidderminster service awaiting departure on 10th September 1949. This bay extended northwards beyond the up main platform, which ended just beyond the passenger footbridge. The goods shed can be seen at the north end of the down platform; it was formally closed in the autumn of 1963 along with the rest of the freight facilities. After this time, all traffic was collected and delivered by road from Hereford, which had previously transhipped the sundries consignments to and from railway vans. Full load traffic was now also concentrated at Hereford. A northbound train was signalled on the up main. H.C. CASSERLEY

by 1900. An Up Refuge siding was added opposite the junction around 1875.

The station was remodelled in 1889 into the shape in which it survived until closure. The up platform was extended southwards to the same length as the down, and a new up bay platform was constructed on the northern end, though set back so that it did not present a face to the Up Main. In addition to the bay line, a run-round road and a repositioned Refuge siding were also provided with room for 32 wagons, engine and van.

Two new sidings were added in the goods yard. A Down Refuge siding was also provided north of the junction, accommodating a train of 40 wagons.

As with many such facilities along the line, the Down Refuge siding was converted into a Down Goods Loop at the end of 1941,

whilst a new Up Goods Loop was provided on the opposite side of the mains; both accommodated engine, 65 wagons and brake van.

The tracks serving the bay platform were removed in 1957, and the Up Refuge siding was reinstated in its original position. The branch trains thenceforth used the main platforms, as they had done in the early years.

Woofferton station closed on 31st July 1961, as did the Tenbury Wells branch, whilst the Down Goods Loop reverted into a Down Refuge siding in that year. Goods services were withdrawn in October 1963, with yard facilities and sidings removed. The Up Refuge siding in the bay was removed in 1964.

The south end of Woofferton Jcn. station, seen from the Comberton road overbridge c.1953. This photograph gives a view of the ends of the bay platform road and sidings as well as the main structures around the station. Its branch connections gave it an enhanced status, with semi-fast and parcels trains calling in addition to the seven main line and various auto services in each direction.

P.J. GARLAND

The 4.30 p.m. Auto (or Rail Motor as it was by now termed) to Tenbury Wells standing alongside the north end of the down platform behind Leominster 0-4-2T No. 1455 on 7th April 1960. This train had arrived as the 4.15 p.m. Ludlow, and after two return trips to Tenbury would run up to Craven Arms before working her final leg of the day back to Leominster.

R.O. TUCK

Shrewsbury Caprotti Standard class '5' 4-6-0 No. 73125 at Woofferton Jct. with the 6.25 p.m. stopping service from Shrewsbury to Hereford on Whit Monday, 10th June 1957. This train called at all thirteen intermediate stations and halts from Dorrington to Leominster, then ran non-stop to Hereford.
MICHAEL MENSING

Kidderminster '57XX' No. 4641 arriving at the down platform, Woofferton, with the 6.25 p.m. Kidderminster on Whit Monday, 10th June 1957. The tail end of the 6.25 p.m. Shrewsbury to Hereford was ahead of the Kidderminster train, providing a connecting service. In this sequence, the 6.25 p.m. Shrewsbury was due at 7.36 p.m., and the Kidderminster (scheduled for a diesel) before it, at 7.30, which does not seem to have occurred in this instance.

MICHAEL MENSING

After the departure of the 6.25 p.m. Shrewsbury, No.4641 probably propelled her stock back onto the branch, ran round the empty coaches, and is pictured here shunting them back into the down platform at Woofferton to work the 7.50 p.m. return service to Kidderminster on 10th June 1957. This service was usually an ex-GWR diesel, but perhaps the bank holiday traffic required more accommodation than those units were able to offer, and an engine and coaches were substituted.

MICHAEL MENSING

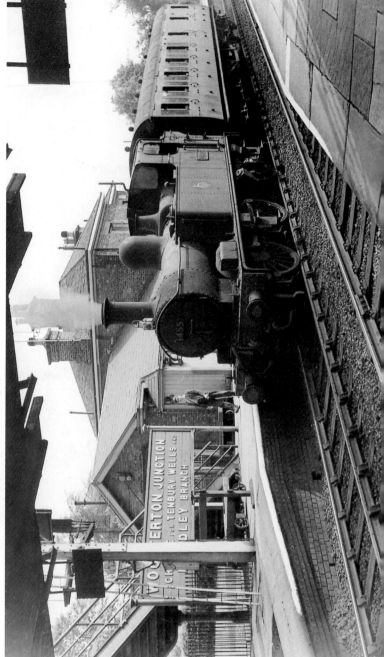

The main station building on the Down side, seen in 1961. As was the case with many such stations, the building contained accommodation for the stationmaster as well as the usual booking hall, waiting room and toilets.

R.S. CARPENTER

Hereford/Leominster 0-4-2T No. 1455 with the one-coach rail-motor from Tenbury Wells at Woofferton down platform on 4th June 1960. By this time, the trailer in use was one of the converted non-corridor Van Thirds. The auto service between Woofferton and Tenbury was withdrawn in July 1961, as were the intermediate main line auto movements.

F.K. DAVIES/
GREAT WESTERN TRUST

Canton 'Castle' No.7023 *Penrice Castle* calling at Woofferton with the 11.10 a.m. Hereford to Shrewsbury local passenger on 10th September 1949. This was not a task that demanded the use of a 'Castle', but was rather a filling-in leg between two express duties. The engine started with the 8.30 a.m. Cardiff to Birmingham train as far as Hereford (due 10.2 a.m.), then took the 11.10 a.m. local on to Shrewsbury, followed by the 12.15 p.m. Manchester (2.25 p.m. Shrewsbury) to Bristol.
H.C. CASSERLEY

Arriving at the south end of Woofferton up platform, No. 1455 is pictured on the 3.50 p.m. Leominster to Ludlow on 5th June 1959. Station gardens were at one time a source of great pride, with prizes offered in divisional competitions; clearly, Woofferton's garden had received some loving attention.
R.O. TUCK

118

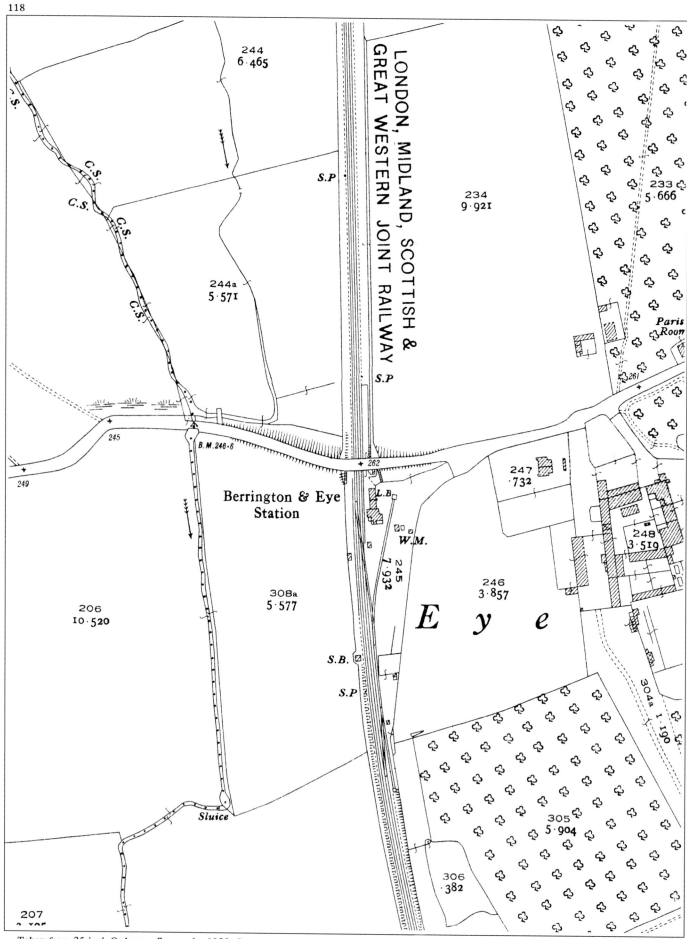

244
6·465

C.S.

C.S.

C.S.

C.S.

C.S.

244a
5·571

S.P

LONDON, MIDLAND, SCOTTISH & GREAT WESTERN JOINT RAILWAY

234
9·921

S.P

233
5·666

Paris
Room

·261

245

249

B.M.246·6

262

247
·732

L.B

Berrington & Eye
Station

W.M.

245
7·932

248
3·519

206
10·520

308a
5·577

246
3·857

E y e

S.B.

S.P

305
5·904

Sluice

306
·382

304a 1·190

207

Taken from 25-inch Ordnance Survey for 1928. Crown copyright reserved.

BERRINGTON & EYE

Berrington & Eye station (at 35m 20ch) was located on the western outskirts of the village of Eye, to the south of the bridge carrying the Ashton to Luston road, though some distance from Berrington Hall, its other namesake. Its original, slightly offset platforms permitted a compact site which included a small single-track goods yard with cattle pens, with trailing connections to each running line.

A signal box was opened in 1875 on the up side.

The down platform was extended northwards by 1890, and the up platform similarly by 1923, but was subsequently shortened.

Berrington & Eye was closed for passenger traffic on 8th June 1958, and to goods services in January 1960. The box is believed to have closed in 1957, when the connections between the Up Main and goods yard were removed, although the southern connection was maintained by a new ground frame. The surviving yard trackwork was taken out of use in early 1961.

A late 1950s view of Berrington & Eye station, with Longsight 'Jubilee' No. 45587 *Beroda* preparing to call with a Shrewsbury to Hereford 4-coach local. The parapet of the road overbridge had been rebuilt in brick, but the arch work still remained in the original stone.

W.A. CAMWELL, STEPHENSON LOCOMOTIVE SOCIETY COLLECTION

Leominster shed, looking north on 24th July 1951, with Nos.1455 and 5807 in the yard. The coaling stage and 45ft turntable were on the sidings to the right of the shed, with a water crane at the yard throat. Although covered accommodation was limited, the two shed roads were quite long, around 100 yards in length.

R.C. RILEY/TRANSPORT TREASURY

Leominster engine shed, a sub-shed of Hereford, is seen here on 4th June 1960, with the only occupant 0-6-0PT No.7426. The two-road, brick-built shed had a 'northlight' pattern roof, with a capacity for only a couple of tank engines on each track; during the war and postwar era, with five locomotives allocated, inside accommodation was tight

F.K. DAVIES/
GREAT WESTERN TRUST

LEOMINSTER

The approach to Leominster engine shed, looking north from just beyond the station in July 1959. The shed, opened in 1901 to replace another to the south of the station, was located on the eastern side of the running lines in this secluded spot alongside the River Lugg, and is seen here about three years before closure.

H.C. CASSERLEY

The second intermediate town of significance on the Shrewsbury & Hereford route was Leominster (38m 38ch), the station at which was located on the eastern outskirts of the town, and opened for traffic on 6th December 1853. At first it was just another through station, though it would increase in importance and expand considerably as a junction as the century progressed.

The first adjustment came for the opening of the Leominster & Kington Railway, which became operational on 2nd August 1857; this joined the S&H route at Kington Jct., a half-mile to the north of the station, as a double junction, extended. A loop around the outer (eastern) face of the Down (now island) platform served the branch trains for Kington, and this was also connected to the S&H engine shed just to the south of that platform.

On the opposite side, to the south of the Up platform, was the goods shed and yard. This comprised a storage siding alongside the Up Main, and another to its west, running through the goods shed. A cattle pen/loading bank was located between the platform end and the goods shed, with two faces at right-angles, one fed from a wagon turntable, a feature that was to be found at other stations on the line. There were two other yard mileage sidings to the west of the shed, with interconnecting roads between wagon turntables. The yard was provided with trailing connections to Up and Down Mains.

At the south end of the complex was Eaton Level Crossing, which took the Bromyard and Worcester road across the railway. This was replaced by an overbridge some time between 1869 and 1875.

The Kington branch itself became more extensive in 1874/5 with the provision of new lines between Titley and Presteign, and Titley and Eardisley (Midland Railway), as well as the extension from Kington to New Radnor.

Two signal boxes were now apparent. The Station box was in an elevated position to the south of the Down platform, spanning the Kington branch platform loop, a recently-added siding and the engine shed roads. To the south of the new Worcester road overbridge was South End box, sitting between the Down Main and the Steens Bridge line.

A new Up Refuge siding joining the Up Main line at South End box was provided.

Another major change to Leominster station occurred in 1884 with the opening of the Leominster & Bromyard Railways branch to Steens Bridge, which approached the station from the south as an independent line running to the east of the main lines. Insofar as Leominster station was concerned, this was accompanied by the provision of a second island platform to the east of the existing one, with connections continued northwards onto the main lines (at Bromyard Jct. box), and one to the Kington platform loop.

A further siding had been laid in the Down yard to the south of the station.

Further modifications had been made by 1897, including a south-wards-extension of the Up platform, and a two-spur arrangement running behind it, the westernmost now serving the loading dock/cattle pens. A third mileage siding was provided in the goods yard, and a third siding in the set on the Down side. The goods yard headshunt was extended southwards alongside the Up Refuge siding, with a connection between them.

In that year, the branch to Steens Bridge was extended to Bromyard, where it joined with the old Worcester, Bromyard & Leominster Railway's line, and through running to Worcester commenced.

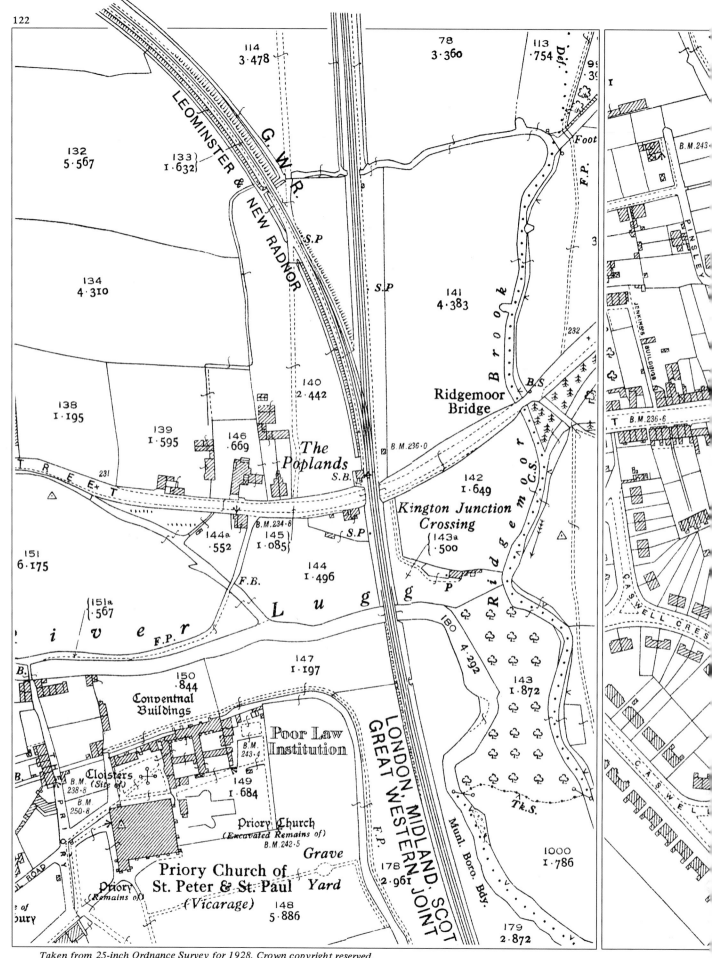

114
3·478

78
3·360

113
·754

Def.

99
39

I

B.M.243

LEOMINSTER & NEW RADNOR

G. W. R.

132
5·567

133
1·632

Foot

F.P.

PINSLEY

JENKINS'S BUILDINGS

S.P

134
4·310

141
4·383

B
r
o
o
k

S.P

B.M.236·6

231

STREET

138
1·195

139
1·595

146
·669

140
2·442

The Poplands

Ridgemoor
Bridge

B.S

142
1·649

C.S.

232

R
i
d
g
e
m
o
o
r

T

CASWELL CRES.

B.M.236·0

S.B.

*Kington Junction
Crossing*

151
6·175

144a
·552

145
1·085

B.M.234·8

S.P

144
1·496

143a
·500

P

151a
·567

F.B.

L   u   g

i   v   e

F.P.

r

B.

147
1·197

180
4·292

143
1·872

150
·844

*Conventual
Buildings*

Poor Law
Institution

B.M.
243·4

LONDON MIDLAND. SCOT.
GREAT WESTERN JOINT

1000
1·786

B.

Cloisters
(Site of)

B.M.
238·8

B.M.
250·8

149
1·684

PRIORY ROAD

Tk.S.

Munl. Boro. Bdy.

Priory Church
(Excavated Remains of)
B.M.242·5

Grave

F.P.

178
2·961

**Priory Church of
St. Peter & St. Paul**
(Vicarage)

Priory
(Remains of)

of
ury

Yard

148
5·886

179
2·872

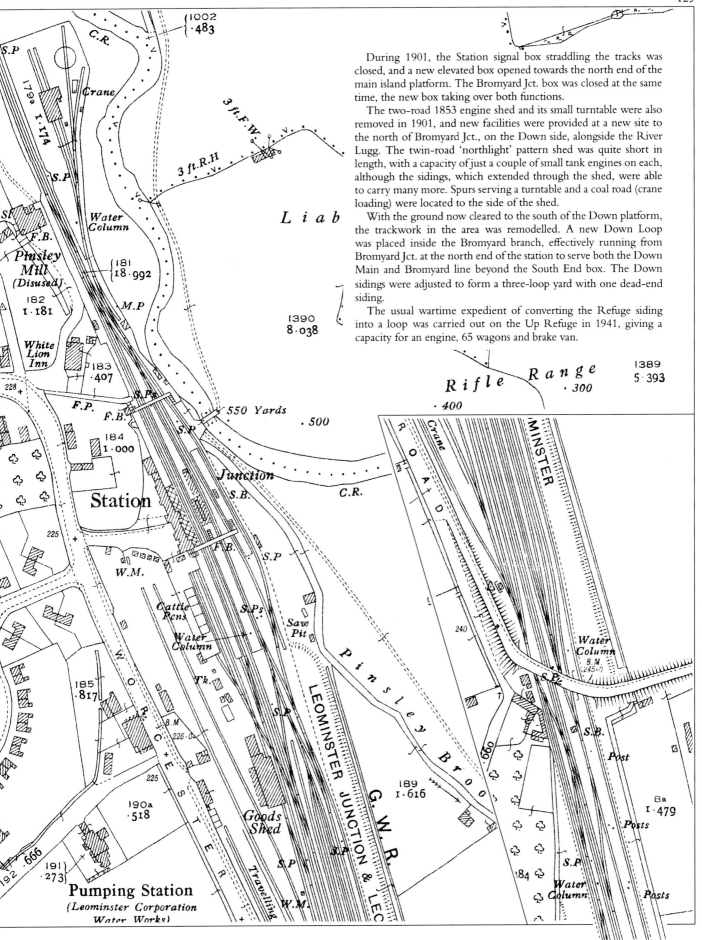

During 1901, the Station signal box straddling the tracks was closed, and a new elevated box opened towards the north end of the main island platform. The Bromyard Jct. box was closed at the same time, the new box taking over both functions.

The two-road 1853 engine shed and its small turntable were also removed in 1901, and new facilities were provided at a new site to the north of Bromyard Jct., on the Down side, alongside the River Lugg. The twin-road 'northlight' pattern shed was quite short in length, with a capacity of just a couple of small tank engines on each, although the sidings, which extended through the shed, were able to carry many more. Spurs serving a turntable and a coal road (crane loading) were located to the side of the shed.

With the ground now cleared to the south of the Down platform, the trackwork in the area was remodelled. A new Down Loop was placed inside the Bromyard branch, effectively running from Bromyard Jct. at the north end of the station to serve both the Down Main and Bromyard line beyond the South End box. The Down sidings were adjusted to form a three-loop yard with one dead-end siding.

The usual wartime expedient of converting the Refuge siding into a loop was carried out on the Up Refuge in 1941, giving a capacity for an engine, 65 wagons and brake van.

Newport Ebbw Junction's WD 2-8-0 No.90573 at Bromyard Jct. on the approach to Leominster station with a southbound class 'H' goods on 20th September 1951. Around the curve beyond the rear of the train was the level crossing with the A49 trunk road, immediately beyond which was Kington Jct., where the New Radnor branch diverged westwards from the main lines. Just behind the engine was the site of the former Bromyard Jct. signal box, situated just to the east of the later engine shed road, and closed in 1901.

T.J. EDGINGTON

The north end of Leominster station at around 12.18 p.m. on Tuesday, 24th July 1951, with Newton Abbot 'Castle' No. 7000 *Viscount Portal* making her way home with the 9.5 a.m. Liverpool to Plymouth service. The engine had worked northwards the previous day with the 8.0 a.m. Plymouth, a turn that the shed also worked on Wednesdays and Fridays of each week. The station nameboard reflects the withdrawal of branch services made in the previous February, with 'New Radnor' and 'Presteign' painted over.

R.C. RILEY/TRANSPORT TREASURY

Rundown of branch passenger services commenced early at Leominster with the closure of the New Radnor and Presteign sections to passengers in 1951, though Kington's trains remained until February 1955. Freight continued over those branches into the mid-1960s. Total closure of the branch to Bromyard took place in September 1952, the line between the station and South End being converted into a siding.

The removal of facilities commenced in earnest during 1962 and, apart from the passenger station and the refuges at South End, all had gone by late 1968.

Leominster station, taken from the public footbridge on 27th June 1950, looking south along the main lines. The main station building is seen to the right, on the up main platform, with two island platforms to its left serving the down main and the three branch roads. The elevated signal box over the centre platforms dominated the station. Facilities on the platforms reduced away from the main, with waiting rooms on the centre island, but only a shelter on the outer branch island to the left.   T.C. COLE

Worcester '57XX' 0-6-0PT No.7750 arriving at the north end of Leominster island platform with a two-coach train (plus van) to form the 12.20 p.m. Leominster to Bromyard and Worcester (Shrub Hill) service on Tuesday, 27th June 1950. It was not until 5th January of that year that A.S. Quatermaine, the Chief Engineer, certified that the '57XXs' had been reclassified as 'Yellow' route engines; they were then officially able to operate over the Bromyard line. Despite this, '57XXs' were noted on branch passenger trains during the war.
          T.C. COLE

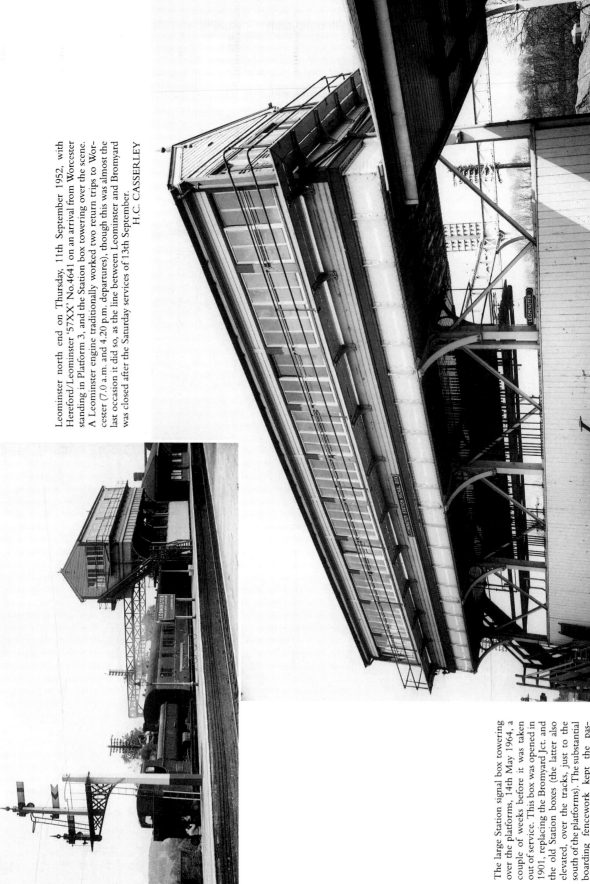

Leominster north end on Thursday, 11th September 1952, with Hereford/Leominster '57XX' No.4641 on an arrival from Worcester standing in Platform 3, and the Station box towering over the scene. A Leominster engine traditionally worked two return trips to Worcester (7.0 a.m. and 4.20 p.m. departures), though this was almost the last occasion it did so, as the line between Leominster and Bromyard was closed after the Saturday services of 13th September.
H.C. CASSERLEY

The large Station signal box towering over the platforms, 14th May 1964, a couple of weeks before it was taken out of service. This box was opened in 1901, replacing the Bromyard Jct. and the old Station boxes (the latter also elevated, over the tracks, just to the south of the platforms). The substantial boarding fencework kept the passengers away from the rodding and wires dropping from the box.
NATIONAL RAILWAY MUSEUM

Leominster station, facing north, viewed from the southern end of the up main platform on 11th September 1952. The passenger footbridge features in the foreground, with that carrying the public right of way across the railway at the far end of the platforms.
H.C. CASSERLEY

The 3.0 p.m. Liverpool to Cardiff express behind Canton 'Castle' No.5089 *Westminster Abbey* passing through Leominster on Monday, 6th August 1951. None of the North & West expresses were scheduled to call at any intermediate station between Shrewsbury and Hereford, and a few did not even call at the latter.   B.W.L. BROOKSBANK/INITIAL PHOTOGRAPHICS

Leominster, looking south towards Hereford from the passenger footbridge on Tuesday, 24th July 1951. The 2.5 p.m. Kington to Leominster arrival – No.1455 and a 'B' set – is seen at the central island branch platform. The starting signal just to the right of the engine was 'off', and indicates 'DN SDS' (down sidings), probably for the empty stock to move into them. A lengthy down goods train behind an ex-LNW 0-8-0, may be seen on the down goods loop in the middle distance; this may have worked through the station alongside the small island platform. The site of the old elevated Station signal box was just to the south of the island platform, over the line connecting the branch with the down main, replaced in 1901 by that over the platform. Beyond this was the original two-road engine shed and turntable, again closed in 1901. The A44 overbridge carrying the Bromyard road can be seen in the distance. R.C. RILEY/TRANSPORT TREASURY

A portrait of 'Castle' No.5073 *Blenheim* at the down main platform on 24th July 1951. The Coleham engine was working the 1.15p.m. Shrewsbury to Hereford local passenger, and appears to have a coloured background to the cab number and nameplates. The engine on this turn was scheduled to work back to Shrewsbury with the 4.20 p.m. local passenger from Hereford, and then take up the Dorrington milk to Banbury. '14XX' No.1455 on the 2.5 p.m. Kington may be seen beyond the 'Castle'.

R.C. RILEY/TRANSPORT TREASURY

The south end of Leominster, looking towards Hereford on 15th May 1963, showing the South End box (some 550 yards from the elevated Station box), taken from the A44 overbridge. '14XX' 0-4-2T No.1458 was probably engaged in shunting work in the goods yard (to the north of the bridge), with the two headshunt/sidings in the foreground. Beyond the mains to the right of the box, the down goods loop converged with the down main, whilst a headshunt/siding ran straight on. The former Bromyard branch (closed in September 1952, and now an extended siding) is seen running along the background in front of the telegraph poles.

B.J. ASHWORTH

The goods facilities at Leominster, looking north from the Bromyard road (A44) bridge, with the goods shed and sidings to the left, on the up side, and the four-road down sidings to the right, beyond the mains. On the far side of these sidings, which appear to have been accommodating an Engineer's train, was the down goods loop, and beyond it – the east-ernmost (far) track – the former Bromyard branch. No.1420 was shunting the goods yard on 13th August 1963, by which time only goods services to Kington and Presteign survived on Leominster's branches.

B.W.L. BROOKSBANK/INITIAL PHOTOGRAPHICS

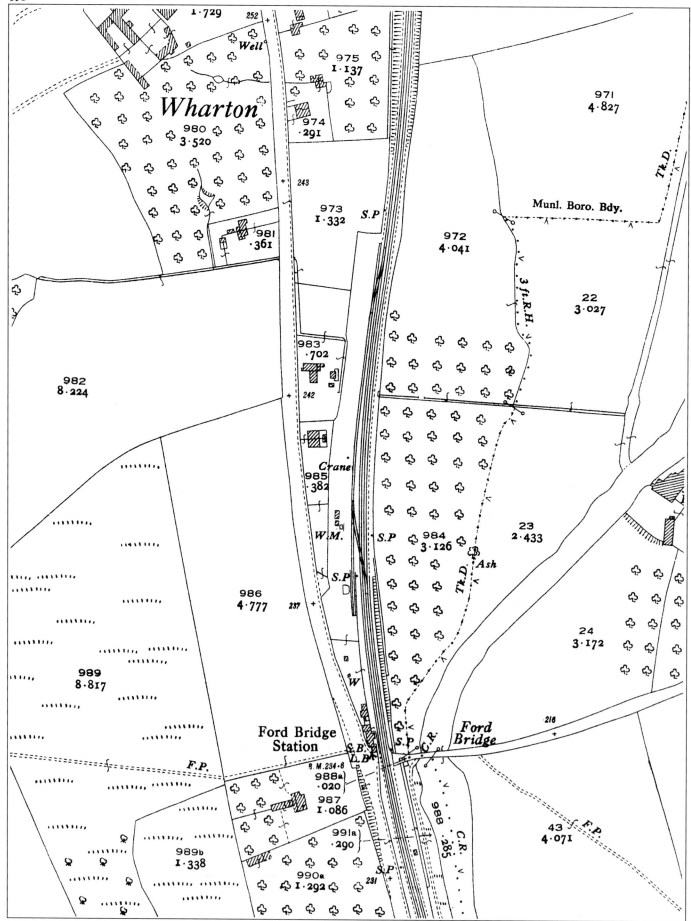

1·729
252
Well
975
1·137
971
4·827

Wharton
980
3·520
974
·291

Tk.D.

973
1·332
S.P
Munl. Boro. Bdy.

243

972
4·041

981
·361

3 ft. R.H.

22
3·027

982
8·224

242

983
·702

Crane
985
·382

23
2·433

W.M.
S.P
984
3·126
Ash

989
8·817

986
4·777
237

S.P

Tk.D.

24
3·172

W

216
Ford Bridge
Station
S.B.
L.B.
S.P
C.R.
Ford Bridge

F.P.
B.M.234·6
988a
·020

988
C.R.
·285

F.P.

989b
1·338
987
1·086

991a
·290

43
4·071

990a
1·292
231
S.P

FORD BRIDGE

Ford Bridge station (at 40m 64ch) was located alongside the A49 trunk road, a little to the south of the village of Wharton, at the point where the minor road to Stoke Prior crossed the River Lugg. The original station comprised two platforms with a level crossing for the Stoke Prior road at the south end, controlled from a signal box at the end of the Up platform.

In 1890, the platforms were extended northwards, and a goods siding installed on the Up side to the north of the station with a trailing connection to each running line.

Ford Bridge was closed on 5th April 1954, one of the earliest stations to close on the line.

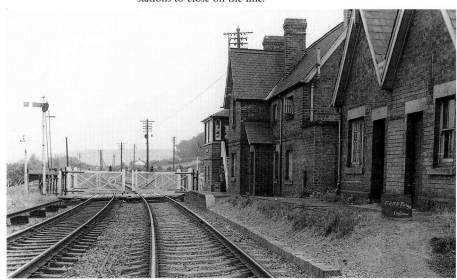

Ford bridge, looking south, with the main buildings to the right, on the Up side, taken in the late 1950s. The signal box controlling the crossing can be seen beyond the station buildings, with the gates in the process of moving. LENS OF SUTTON

The up side of Ford Bridge, looking north in June 1950, showing the main station buildings. This view was taken from the level crossing with a minor road to Stoke Prior. A modest goods yard comprising a single siding with spurs was located beyond the north end of the up platform, alongside the A49 road. T.C. COLE

Approaching the north end of Dinmore Tunnel, Shrewsbury 'Castle' No.5050 *Earl of St. Germans* is seen with the 9.10 a.m. Liverpool to Plymouth (with four coaches for Paignton at the head) on the first leg of her double-home working to Newton Abbot on Friday, 2nd July 1954. On her Monday and Wednesday turns, the engine returned the following days with the 8.0 a.m. Plymouth from Newton, but in this instance, her duty would be the 8.45 a.m. Plymouth on the much busier Saturday. She is seen passing the village of Hope under Dinmore, which gave its name to the former Hope Crossing (on the curve under the train, closed when the line was doubled in 1893), as well as the 1,051-yard tunnels.

R.O. TUCK

At the north end of Dinmore Tunnel, Shrewsbury '7F' (class G2a) 0-8-0 No.49260 is seen emerging with an up class 'H' goods service on 2nd July 1954, probably from Pontypool Road. The old tunnel (on the left here), serving the down line, was on a gradient that fell continuously at 1 in 100 from the northern portal to a point south of the station, a mile away. Opened in 1893, the new tunnel (serving the new up line) was on a different profile, near the top of a 1 in 135 climb that stretched for around 1½ miles (though flattening a little through Dinmore station), giving up trains a rather less arduous climb than hitherto.   R.O. TUCK

DINMORE

As the railway headed south from Ford Bridge alongside the River Lugg, it was confronted with a sharp 'U' bend in the valley as the river skirted a spur of higher ground, Dinmore Hill. The decision was taken to instigate a gentle climb along the contours on the west side of the valley and to tunnel through the hill with a single bore from a point to the south of Hope under Dinmore, with a 1 in 100 fall of some 1¼ miles through the tunnel (1,051 yards) and back into the widening valley of the Lugg.

The original station (at 43m 42ch) was located on the southern side of the hill, a short distance from the portal of the tunnel at the recommencement of the double-track width. A small yard of three sidings, and a signal box, were positioned on the down side, immediately to its south.

Dinmore tunnel was becoming a considerable bottleneck for traffic by the 1890s, and it was decided to provide a second bore, to the

west of the first, serving an independent Up line. The line through the old tunnel now became the Down. In order to ease the gradient for northbound trains, the climb was started at about two miles from the summit at the north end of the tunnel, allowing gradients of around 1 in 135 throughout, with a short section of easing at the station's new Up platform. The tunnel was opened to traffic in late 1893.

This arrangement gave a curious look to the station, where the two platforms were widely separated, and at different heights, with the Up some eight feet higher than the Down.

The station was closed to passengers on 9th June 1958, and to goods six years later. The signal box was taken out of use in 1958, and a ground frame provided to operate the goods yard connections; this was removed when the yard closed in 1964.

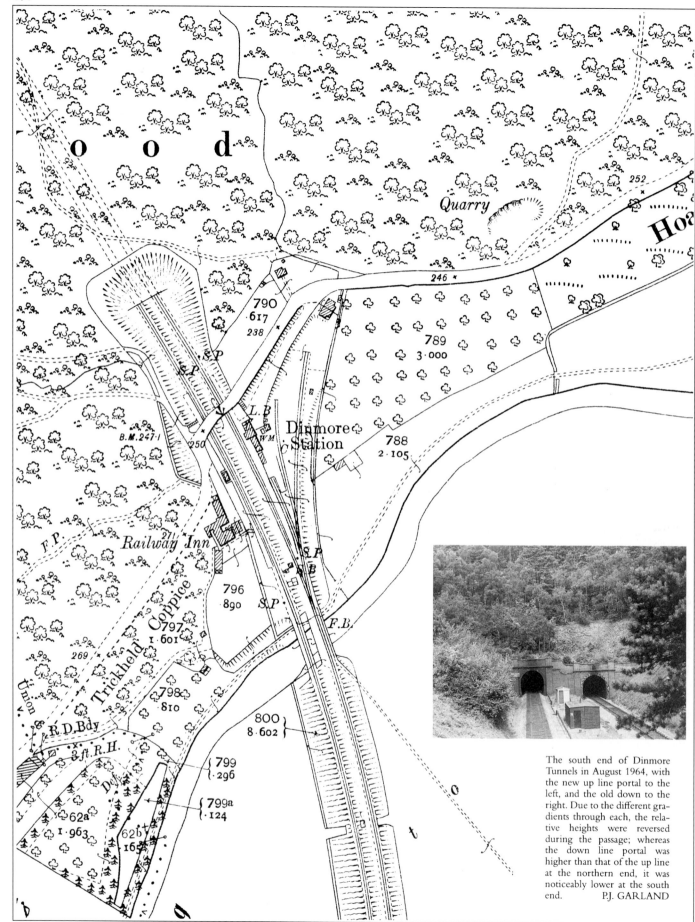

The south end of Dinmore Tunnels in August 1964, with the new up line portal to the left, and the old down to the right. Due to the different gradients through each, the relative heights were reversed during the passage; whereas the down line portal was higher than that of the up line at the northern end, it was noticeably lower at the south end.

P.J. GARLAND

Taken from 25-inch Ordnance Survey for 1904. Crown copyright reserved.

Dinmore station on two levels, looking north, showing the southern portals of the new (left, up line) and old (right, down line) tunnels beyond the spans of the road bridge.   LENS OF SUTTON

Dinmore, looking northwards along the track towards the up line portal in August 1964, with the remnants of the 1893 up platform on the left. Dinmore Hill, through which the tunnel passed, is evident in this view. A descending bore through the hill was chosen rather than a deviation to the east to avoid the spur of high ground.

P.J. GARLAND

Seen from the road overbridge, Hereford 'Hall' No.5998 *Trevor Hall* leaving the south end of Dinmore Tunnel on the 1 in 100 falling gradient with the 3.5 p.m. Manchester (Piccadilly) to Plymouth and Paignton on Saturday, 18th August 1962. The train was 'V98', but, like the others shown in the sequence, was not carrying any identification on this day. The notice on the up line portal warned drivers of the runaway catch points, some 500 yards to the rear.   MICHAEL MENSING

The down line at Dinmore, looking north in August 1964, showing part of the goods yard just after closure, and the main station buildings some six years after the withdrawal of passenger services. The Bodenham road overbridge runs behind the station, with its twin arches spanning the separated main lines. This was the original site of the station, with the two main running lines passing together beneath a bridge, a platform to each, before becoming single width for the passage through the tunnel. Beyond is the southern portal of the old tunnel, with the light at the northern end visible.   P.J. GARLAND

Dinmore goods yard sidings throat, looking south in August 1964, showing the now-truncated formation clear of the main line. Obviously, only down goods trains could serve the station after the doubling and station rebuilding of 1893. The up line on the embankment to the right shows the height differential at this point.   P.J. GARLAND

Royal Scot 4-6-0 No. 46129 *The Scottish Horse* passing the site of Dinmore station with the ten-coach 12 noon Kingswear to Manchester Piccadilly on Saturday, 18th August 1962. The train is seen on the short length of 1 in 260 gradient through the station area on the 1-in-135 climb to the north end of Dinmore Tunnel, and would soon enter the southern end of the bore.   MICHAEL MENSING

Canton 'Castle' No.5081 *Lockheed Hudson* would shortly enter Dinmore Tunnel with the 4.40 p.m. Cardiff to Liverpool service on Saturday, 18th August 1962. The photograph was taken from the overbridge carrying the minor road to Bodenham, and shows the retaining wall that at one time backed the up platform, with the alcove that once contained the waiting shelter.
MICHAEL MENSING

138

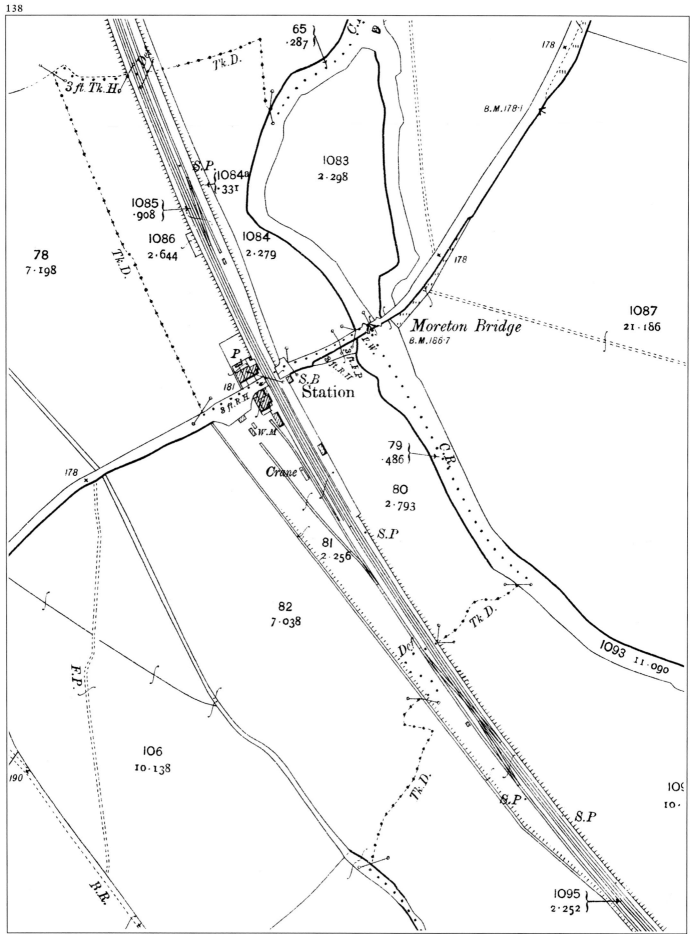

MORETON-ON-LUGG

Moreton-on-Lugg station, looking north from the middle of the up platform towards the main station buildings, level crossing and signal box, in March 1958. The previous signal box had been to the south of the crossing gates, but was replaced by that shown in 1943. In that year, new MoD sidings were built on the up side of the line beyond the crossing, whilst the existing down refuge siding on the opposite side of the mains was converted into a loop having a capacity of 70 wagons (in addition to engine and brake van).
R.M. CASSERLEY

The down platform at Moreton-on-Lugg, looking towards Hereford, viewed from an up train in August 1954. The brick-built shelter was located around the middle of the down platform. Behind the train may just be seen the points leading into the goods yard, located behind the up platform, whilst an up refuge siding (again for 70 wagons) extended from it around the outside of the curve.
H.C. CASSERLEY

Moreton-on-Lugg station (at 46m 68ch) was located alongside the River Lugg, about a half-mile to the east of the Moreton village at the point where the road to Marden crossed both railway and river. The station originally had a Down platform with a signal box at its north end, and a rather shorter Up platform to permit a small siding and spur on that side, connected only to the Up Main. A level crossing ran across the tracks at the north end of the station.

A Down Refuge siding was added around 1895 to the north of the level crossing, whilst around the turn of the century, the main goods siding was extended southwards and provided with a trailing connection to the Down Main. A second mileage siding was also added, along with a small cattle pen.

An Up Refuge siding was constructed as a southwards-extension to the main yard siding, though with its own connection to the Up Main made beyond a section usable as a headshunt for the yard.

In 1943, the Ministry of Defence opened an extensive Royal Army Ordnance Depot on the up side, to the north of the level crossing. Connected to Up and Down Mains at both ends, it comprised five loop sidings parallel to the main line, with the lead into the depot at their north end. The depot itself had a nest of six loop sidings just inside the entrance, which fanned out into five separate nests of sidings for loading and unloading. There were three main sheds with siding access and storage between, and a small engine shed for the depot shunter.

Also in 1943, the Down Refuge siding was converted into a Down Goods Loop, with accommodation for engine, 70 wagons and brake.

The additional facilities required a new signal box, which was provided to the north of the level crossing on the down side. The old box was removed.

Moreton's passenger services were withdrawn on 9th June 1958, and goods in September 1964. The MoD depot survived the passing of the steam age.

HEREFORD

The city of Hereford had a quite complex arrangement of railways, in which five main companies originally had an interest. The original ownership was:

Shrewsbury & Hereford: southwards through to Barrs Court South Jct.
Worcester & Hereford: westwards to Shelwick Jct. (and Barrs Court North Jct. to Barton station, though built by NA&H))
Newport, Abergavenny & Hereford: southwards from Barrs Court North Jct.
Hereford, Ross & Gloucester: southwards from Barrs Court South Jct.
Hereford, Hay & Brecon (Midland): eastwards to Barton (Moorfields)

Thus, the line from Shrewsbury to Barrs Court Jct. South (11 chains to the south of Barrs Court station) was S&H and was

nominally 'connected' there with the HR&G line from Gloucester. However, this was not so in practice, as the Gloucester line was then to the broad-gauge; the S&H had standard gauge arrangements at the north part of Barrs Court station, and the HR&G broad gauge at the south.

To the north and west of the city, the line from Bans Court North Jct. (later Barrs Court Jct.) southwards to Barton and beyond was NA&H, though the section between Barrs Court North and Barton station was W&H, but constructed by the NA&H as agents. The two became one as part of the West Midland company in July 1860.

The line to the south of the Barrs Court station area was laid to broad gauge for the HR&G (which amalgamated with the Great Western in July 1862), but in 1866 the L&NW built a standard gauge connecting link from a point 1¼ miles to the south of Barrs Court

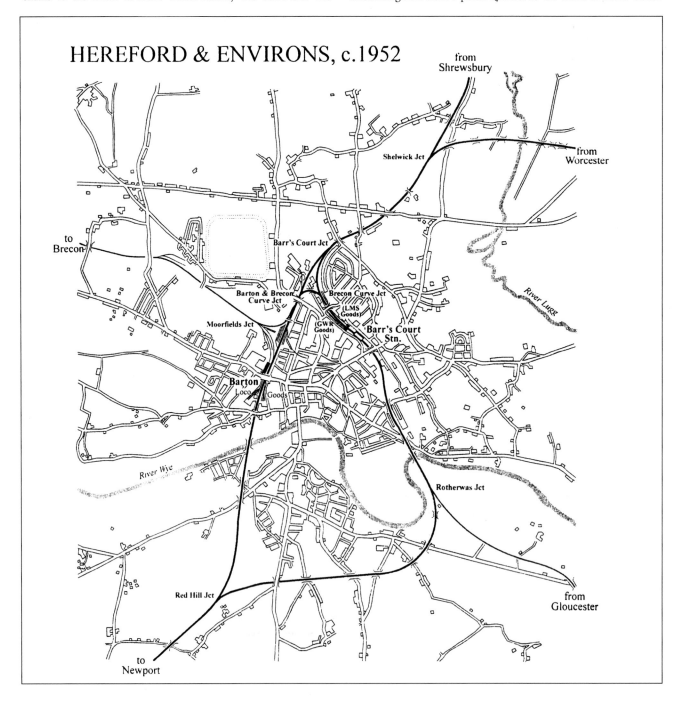

HEREFORD & ENVIRONS, c.1952

station (Rotherwas Jct.) some two miles south-westwards to join the route from Barton to Abergavenny at Red Post Jct. (1½ miles south of Barton), which completed the railway 'circle' around the city. To provide access to this link for standard gauge trains, the broad gauge line between Barrs Court station and Rotherwas Jct. was converted to mixed gauge track, opened on 16th July 1866.

By this time, the writing was on the wall for the broad gauge, and on 14th August 1869 the broad gauge was removed from Hereford, whilst the branch from Rotherwas Jct. to Grange Court was similarly converted to standard gauge over the following week.

All the individualities at Hereford were, of course, consumed in the various amalgamations, and by late 1870 the various lines were Great Western, London & North Western, GW and L&NW Joint, or Midland-owned. From 1922, this was further reduced to the Great Western and London, Midland & Scottish companies, or Joint.

The HH&B had opened to Moorfields in 1862, though the passenger station was closed in April 1874, and Midland trains thereafter used Barton station.

In January 1893, the final part of the railway map was created with the opening of the Brecon Curves and the subsequent closure of Barton station, leaving Barrs Court as the only passenger station. All passenger traffic from the three companies (with the very occasional exception of some non-stop services in earlier years) thus utilised Barrs Court from that time.

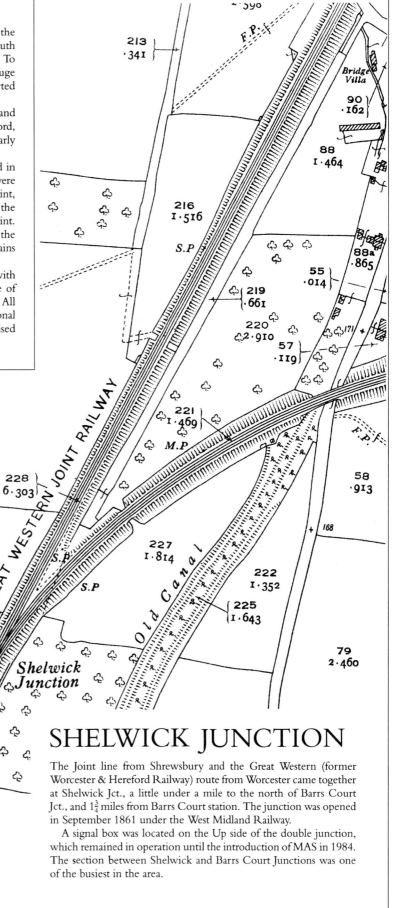

SHELWICK JUNCTION

The Joint line from Shrewsbury and the Great Western (former Worcester & Hereford Railway) route from Worcester came together at Shelwick Jct., a little under a mile to the north of Barrs Court Jct., and 1¾ miles from Barrs Court station. The junction was opened in September 1861 under the West Midland Railway.

A signal box was located on the Up side of the double junction, which remained in operation until the introduction of MAS in 1984. The section between Shelwick and Barrs Court Junctions was one of the busiest in the area.

HEREFORD BARRS COURT JUNCTION

A short down class '8' ('H') freight hauled by Shrewsbury '8F' 2-8-0 No.48404 approaching Hereford Barrs Court Junction on 19th August 1964. It was signalled to take the Barton line for Worcester Sidings, where it would probably have terminated. The centre signals covered the route into Barrs Court station and goods, and the goods signal the lines that forked left just before Barrs Court Jct. itself.
B.J. ASHWORTH

The point at which the lines to Barrs Court and Barton diverged was Barrs Court Jct. (though official references were made to Barton Junction, then Barrs Court North Jct.). It was opened in January 1854, along with the connecting link to Barton, so that traffic between the Shrewsbury & Hereford and the Newport, Abergavenny & Hereford Railways might connect. This they did for a year or so, until the S&H services were diverted back to Barrs Court to connect with the newly-arrived Hereford, Ross & Gloucester company. Shortly afterwards, a platform was built at the junction for interchange of coaches and/or passengers, with a system of Pilot trips serving the three locations. This continued until the completion of the Barton & Brecon Curve in 1893, when Midland Railway services that formerly used Barton station were afforded a direct route into Barrs Court station.

Barrs Court Jct. box was positioned on the Up (west) side of the junction, with the original box replaced in 1878.

The Second World War brought about changes at Barrs Court Jct. with the addition of a second double junction in December 1941 to provide independent goods running lines into Barrs Court goods. The new junction was immediately to the north of the existing one, and the new Up and Down Goods lines ran to the east side of the existing route to Barrs Court station, extending as far as Ayleston Hill box. The first section, to Brecon Curve box, was designated as Refuge Loops, with a 65 (Down) and 41 (Up) wagon capacity, whilst the half-mile or so length beyond could accommodate 'several trains' on each line.

Barrs Court signal box was unusually located on the top of an embankment, between the goods lines and Barrs Court junctions, on the up (west) side of the running lines. This box replaced another on a site alongside it in the late 1870s, and was closed in 1966 upon the removal of the Barton & Brecon Curve, and the goods lines alongside the Barrs Court station route.
R.H. MARROWS

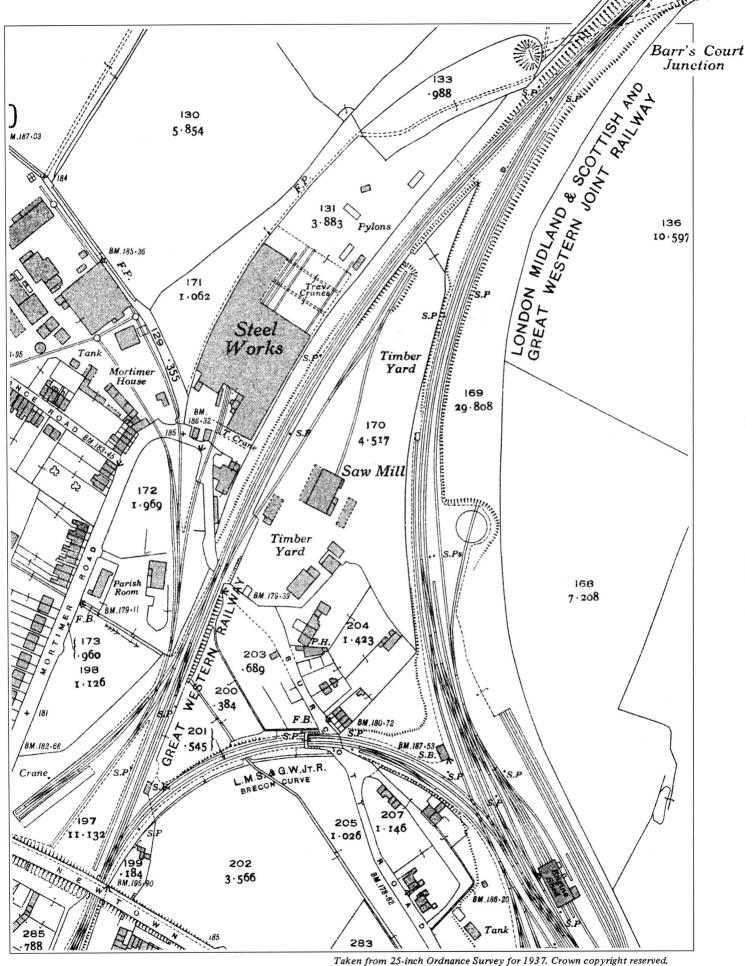

Barr's Court
Junction

LONDON MIDLAND & SCOTTISH AND
GREAT WESTERN JOINT RAILWAY

130
5·854

133
·988

136
10·597

M.187·03

184

BM.185·36

F.P.

F.P.

129 ·355

131
3·883

Pylons

171
1·062

*Trave
Cranes*

**Steel
Works**

S.P

S.P

S.P

S.P

*Timber
Yard*

169
29·808

S.P

Tank

*Mortimer
House*

BM.188·32

185

7. Crane

S.P

170
4·517

Saw Mill

168
7·208

ROAD

BM.183·45

*Timber
Yard*

MORTIMER

172
1·969

*Parish
Room*

BM.179·11

F.B.

173
·960

198
1·126

BM.182·66

181

201
·545

200
·384

203
·689

BM.179·39

204
1·423

P.H.

F.B.

BM.180·72

S.P

S.Ps

S.P

BM.187·53

S.B.

S.P

S.P

Crane

S.P

S.P

S.P

L.M.S. & G.W. JT. R.
BRECON CURVE

S.P

207
1·146

S.P

197
11·132

S.P

199
·184

BM.195·90

NEWTOWN

185

202
3·566

205
1·026

BM.178·62

ROAD

BM.188·20

S.P

285
·788

283

Tank

GREAT WESTERN RAILWAY

Taken from 25-inch Ordnance Survey for 1937. Crown copyright reserved.

BARTON and MOORFIELDS

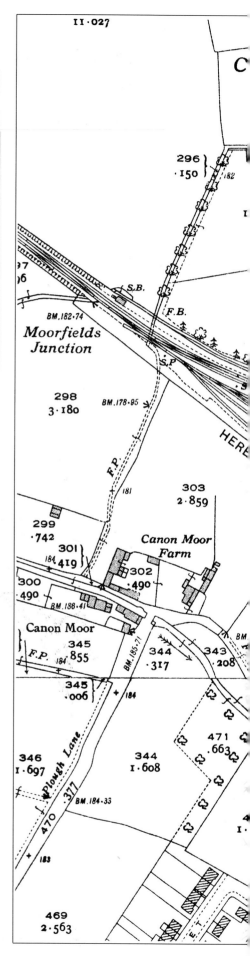

From Barrs Court Jct., the old Worcester & Hereford and Newport, Abergavenny & Hereford Railways' route (and briefly that of the West Midland Railway) headed south past Worcester Sidings, on the Up side, to Barton, their station in the city, before continuing southwards to Abergavenny and Pontypool.

Beyond Worcester Sidings, to the west side of the line, the former Hereford, Hay & Brecon Railway (later Midland) station at Moorfields was located, that railway curving around briefly towards Barton before terminating. Opened at Hereford in October 1862, the line ran initially to Moorhampton, with extensions onwards to Eardisley, Hay and, in September 1864, to Three Cocks Jct. on the new Mid-Wales route. Passenger services from Moorfields station commenced in June 1863. As well as a passenger station, there were goods and locomotive facilities at the terminus.

In August 1866, Barton station saw a great reduction in its Great Western services with the opening of the L&NW's Hereford Curve between the new Rotherwas and Red Hill Junctions, permitting through trains between the North and Newport to utilise Barrs Court station.

Moorfields passenger station was finally closed in April 1874, by which time an independent line had been constructed from Moorfields alongside the Great Western line into Barton station, which the Midland company then used from that time.

The initial layout of Worcester Sidings was five dead-end roads feeding north, access being controlled from Barton No.4 box, with a couple more sidings alongside the Down Main on the opposite side.

In the early 1890s, the decision was made to close Barton station and concentrate all passenger services at Barrs Court. For the Great Western and London & North Western companies this involved little change, but for the Midland company, whose line arrived on the far side of the city, the problems of access were far greater. So, two loop lines were constructed to allow the running of Midland passenger trains from Moorfields to Barrs Court. The first, at Moorfields, took the branch northwards to join with the old Worcester & Hereford section at Hay & Brecon Jct., just to the south of the Newton Road overbridge. On the north side of that bridge, the second loop was constructed as a chord joining the Barton and Barrs Court routes; this left the W&H route at Barton & Brecon Curve Jct., and swung around eastwards to join the Barrs Court (ex-S&H) route at Brecon Curve Jct., from which Midland trains were able to

Barton & Brecon Curve Jct., looking north from the A49 overbridge on 3rd August 1964. This was the junction between the Brecon Curve (opened in 1893, running to Barrs Court, Brecon Curve Jct., and seen curving around to the right) and the 'Hereford & Newport' line (former Worcester & Hereford Railway. though built by the Newport, Abergavenny & Hereford Railway). running straight onwards towards Barrs Court Junction. The curve was used by Midland Railway passenger trains to Hereford following the closure of, first, their own terminus at Moorfields (1874), and then the GWR station at Barton (1893), as well as Great Western loco and goods movements.
P.J. GARLAND

145

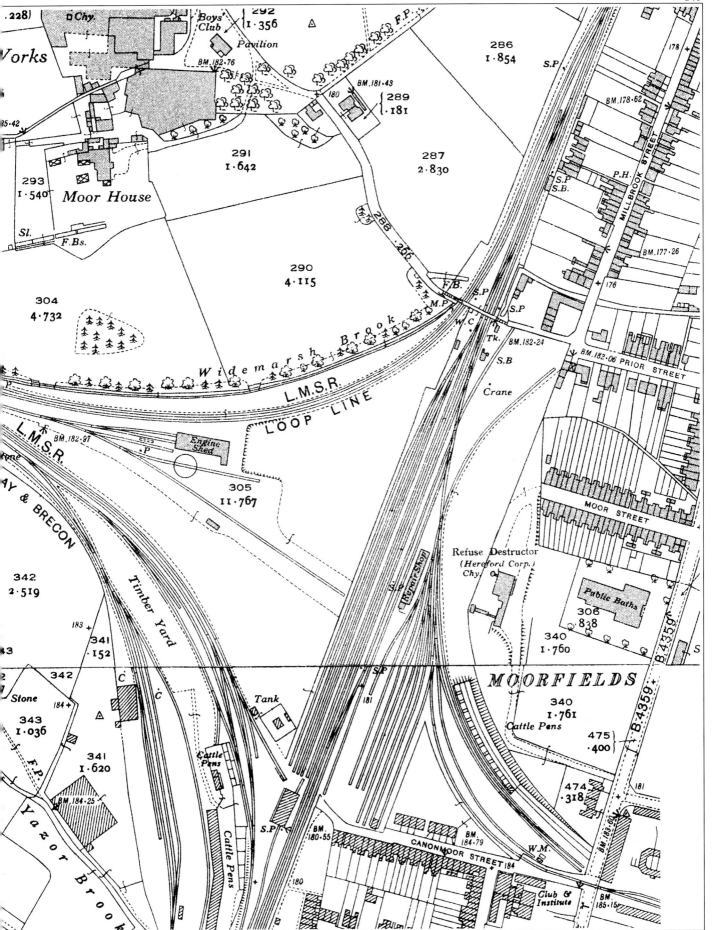

Taken from 25-inch Ordnance Survey for 1937. Crown copyright reserved.

A view from the A49 road overbridge in 1964, looking south towards Barton with Hay & Brecon Jct. in the foreground. The former Midland route to Hay and Three Cocks Jct. (for Brecon, opened 1862-4) diverged to the right, whilst the main line to Barton ran straight on. Barton Curve Jct. signal box to the left of the running lines, is another of the confusing array of names to those unfamiliar with the Hereford railway scene. A public footbridge may be seen in the middle distance.

PJ. GARLAND

Barton Curve Junction box is seen on the right in this view, looking north from the public footbridge towards the A49 road overbridge. The ex-Midland Hay & Brecon line curve (opened in 1893) ran underneath the photographer to join with the Barton line at the junction in front of the road bridge, with the Brecon Curve diverging to the right for Barrs Court immediately beyond it. '16XX' class 0-6-0PT No.1613 is seen working on the Up Worcester Sidings headshunt.

PJ. GARLAND

This view from the public footbridge with the former Midland line from Brecon curving sharply away westwards, shows 0-6-0T No. 1613 waiting for its next movement into Worcester Sidings from the headshunt, on 3rd August 1964. The former Midland engine shed can be seen on the outside of the curve, top left; to its left, off the picture, was the site of the original Midland passenger terminus and goods yard of Moorfields. The Midland line was later extended through to Barton station (1874), and the Midland terminus closed.   P.J. GARLAND

run directly into Barrs Court. The latter loop was also extremely useful for Great Western operations (it was Joint line property) in that it gave a convenient connection between the goods facilities at Barrs Court and those around Barton, as well as locomotive access to Barton loco, without having to run via Barrs Court Jct., with a reversal.

The new loops were opened on 1st January 1893, and Midland trains utilised the route to Barrs Court station the following day. The Midland ceased to use Barton station, which was closed on the same day, 2nd January 1893. Although the connecting line from Moorfields to Barton station thus lost its passenger service, it did remain open for freight movements for a while, before the connection was severed around the turn of the century. The Midland Railway) goods facilities were also expanded in January 1893 with

the opening of a large new goods shed (Moorfields Goods Depot) to the south of the old terminus.

In the twentieth century, Worcester Sidings expanded onto the Down side with a bank of eight short sidings, cattle pen and other roads, as well as private industry. A further six sidings were added to the Up Sidings in 1942; Up and Down goods lines were provided to the outer side of these.

The old two-platform station at Barton, with four tracks through the middle, was retained for goods purposes, and was not actually removed until 1913, though parts of the station survived afterwards.

Rundown of Worcester Sidings commenced in 1966, with the bank of Down sidings being taken out of use in 1968. By 1970, only the eight sidings on the Up side remained, with a small number of the sidings on the Down being retained for the Engineers.

A panoramic view of Worcester Sidings, facing south from the public footbridge. The main line is seen running through the middle, to the left of No.1613 and its wagons in the up sidings. To the right of these were the bi-directional goods loops. The Worcester Down Sidings are seen to the left of the running lines. Beyond the waste ground on the extreme right (and just in front of the storage tanks) is the site of Moorfields terminus, with wagons standing on the remaining goods sidings. In the distance can be seen the Portland Street footbridge.   P.J. GARLAND

Hereford '16XX' 0-6-0PT No.1667 is pictured shunting at Barton on 4th August 1961, believed to be just to the north of the Eign Street overbridge. The shunting truck (DW 41887) was marked as 'Hereford, Worcester Sidings', where it had been since at least 1944. There were two more shunting trucks for the yards at Barrs Court.

F.K. DAVIES/GREAT WESTERN TRUST

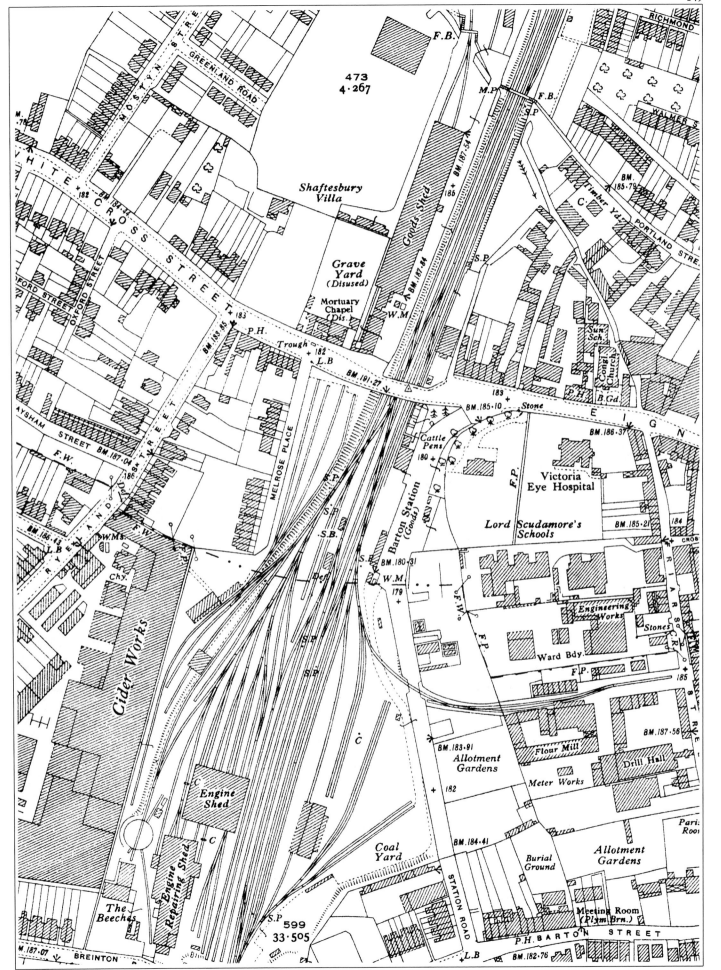

Taken from 25-inch Ordnance Survey for 1937. Crown copyright reserved.

Hereford Barton engine shed forms the backdrop to this picture of a 'Hall' class 4-6-0 on 15th May 1964, which appears to have been shunting a train of coal back into the sidings alongside the shed. The wagons of large coal were probably locomotive coal for the shed and the wagons of small coal, piled high, may have been for the Hereford Gas Works, further up the line. The main shed building is seen behind the rear wagons being shunted, with part of the shops just seen around the corner to its right, and the coal stage on the right. The signal box was Barton. To the left, the warehouses originally formed the down side of Barton station (closed 1893), whilst the up side was just to the right of the 'Hall', with four roads between.   B.J. ASHWORTH

Cardiff East Dock 'Manor' No.7805 *Broome Manor* heading past Barton box on 9th May 1963 with what was probably a Cardiff (Pengam) to Chester (Saltney) or Birmingham (Lawley St.) class '5' ('D') freight, with the usual vacuum head of vans from Cardiff Goods. The large number of 'Vanfits' outwards from Cardiff Goods each day enabled most long-distance freights from Pengan to run with high-priority headcodes.

COLLECTION R.K. BLENCOWE

BARTON SHED

The eight-road Barton shed, seen on 13th May 1951, with '43XXs', 'Halls' and pannier tanks amongst the engines on display. At this time, the shed was home to around 36 engines, including the three 'Saints', five 'Halls', a '28XX', eight '43XXs' and the remainder 0-6-0s, both tender and tank. Although of some width, the shed was only around 135ft in length, which could house two 'Saints' or four tank engines on each road. R.S. CARPENTER

The first company into Hereford was the Shrewsbury & Hereford, on 6th December 1853, worked initially by the line's constructor, Thomas Brassey. His offer to run the line for the company was soon formalized into an agreement whereby, from 1st July 1854, he would operate the line for a period of eight years. Arrangements for engine stabling and maintenance at Hereford in this early period are not known, but some would certainly have been required in the general vicinity of Barrs Court station.

On 2nd January 1854, the Newport, Abergavenny & Hereford commenced operations from Barton station, and two weeks later were connected to the S&H line at Barrs Court North Jct. The company opened an engine shed just to the south of Barton station.

The Hereford, Ross & Gloucester company opened their line at Hereford on 1st June 1855, and established a two-road broad gauge shed just to the south of Barrs Court station, on the Down side against the junction of Aylestone Hill and North Villa Road, immediately behind the site of the later Ayleston Hill signal box.

In July 1862, the S&H was leased jointly to the Great Western, the London & North Western and West Midland companies, and soon afterwards the L&NW constructed a three-road shed near Barrs Court North Jct. on the Down side of the main lines.

With the amalgamation of the Great Western and West Midland companies in August 1863, the shed at Barton became Great Western property, and was thus available for all the company's engine stock.

The HR&G shed was closed in August 1869 with the removal of the broad gauge from Hereford, and the standard gauge branch engines thereafter used Barton shed. The old HR&G building became a carriage shed.

In the late 1890s, Barton comprised an eight-road running shed, with the shops in another building to its south. A coal stage stood to the north of the running shed, and a turntable further still to the

north, near the Up platform at Barton station. In 1909, the turntable was moved to a location to the west of the coal stage.

The earliest available allocation for Hereford is 1901:

Class	Type	Engines
111	2-4-0	373, 374, 1005, 1010,
481	2-4-0	481, 485, 489, 590
2201	2-4-0	2205
3226	2-4-0	3226, 3227
W. Mid	2-4-0	199
Std. Gds	0-6-0	370, 411, 658, 779. 798, 800, 1090
2301	0-6-0	2352, 2416, 2525
850	0-6-0ST	94, 998, 1220. 1939, 2018
1076	0-6-0ST	1147, 1231
1501	0-6-0ST	1552
1854	0-6-0ST	1854
517	0-4-2T	204, 545, 562, 1436, 1437, 1438

Of the above, the 2-4-0s were seen mainly on the Hereford & Birmingham and Hereford & South Wales services, and local passenger trains to Shrewsbury, though with occasional fast turns on North & West trains. Latterly, some of the older engines were also used on the Gloucester line services.

The 0-6-0s were primarily utilised on goods services over all the lines, although they did regularly appear on passenger trains on the Gloucester – and occasionally Worcester – lines.

'517s' were used on local passenger services, including the Gloucester branch, as were some of the 0-6-0Ts on goods. The six-coupled tanks also provided local goods, transfer and shunting power.

Other classes to find their way into the allocation for Hereford shortly after this time included '56' and '378' ('Sir Daniel') class

2-4-0s, and the former Severn & Wye company's 0-6-0T No.1356 *Will Scarlet*.

As the decade progressed. the 2-4-0s were gradually replaced by 4-4-0s initially of the 'Duke' and 'Bulldog' classes (1908/09). In 1907 one of the large-wheel 'City' class, No. 3701 *Gibraltar*, arrived and remained at Hereford until 1914. In 1912 an 'Atbara', No. 3376 (4123 from 28th December 1912) arrived and stayed until 1916.

In 1914. the allocation was:

Class	Type	Engines
City	4-4-0	3701
Atbara	4-4-0	4123
Bulldog	4-4-0	3313, 3368, 3405, 3415, 3425, 3427
481	2-4-0	487, 489
2201	2-4-0	2216, 2218
Std. Gds	0-6-0	116, 392, 403, 404, 427, 500, 513, 608, 609, 801, 875, 891
360	0-6-0	369
850	0-6-0ST	93, 94, 2016
	0-6-0PT	1221
1016	0-6-0ST	1037
1076	0-6-0ST	1147, 1183, 1231
	0-6-0PT	1627
2021	0-6-0ST	2151 2153

The working emphasis of the 4-4-0s was much as had been with the 2-4-0s in the previous decade. Other significant points here were the removal of the '2301' class 0-6-0s, and the replacement by older 'Standard Goods', and the transfer away of the '517s'.

During, the Great War, the 'Bulldog' class allocation rose above ten, with only an occasional large-wheeled 4-4-0 provided (including 'County' class engines). In the latter stages of the conflict, with the 4-6-0s increasingly replacing the 4-4-0s on primary services, a larger selection of the large-wheeled varieties were allocated, and by 1920 'County', 'Badminton', 'Atbara' and 'Flower' classes were to be seen together on shed. Nevertheless, it was the shed's dozen or so 'Bulldogs' that would have the lion's share of passenger turns in the 1920s. Single examples of '26XX' class 2-6-0s were also allocated in this period, with a '43XX' following soon afterwards.

In 1928, the shed's stud of 'Bulldogs' were by far the most common engine at Barton, but additional 'Counties' had also arrived.

'County'	4-4-0	3801, 3824, 3827
'Bulldog'	4-4-0	3301, 3303, 3309, 3317, 3320, 3349, 3355, 3365, 3380, 3383, 3420, 3425, 3433, 3437
43XX	2-6-0	6370
26XX	2-6-0	2622, 2648, 2680
2301	0-6-0	2348, 2401, 2553
2361	0-6-0	2365
645	0-6-0PT	650
850	0-6-0ST	990, 998, 1936, 1937
	0-6-0PT	93, 1919
1076	0-6-0ST	1243
1501	0-6-0ST	1513
2021	0-6-0PT	2080, 2093
2721	0-6-0PT	2777

Again, the '850' and '2021' class contingents were significant at the shed, partly for working over some of the more restricted locations.

The 'Bulldog' rosters were now quite comprehensive, covering all the Great Western lines out of Hereford. One example has survived, and illustrates the varied use of the class:

6.55 Hereford	Gloucester 8.2
8.51 Gloucester	Swindon 10.13
(7.20 Severn Tunnel Jct.)	
11.10 Swindon	Gloucester 12/25
(8.7 Slough)	
2/5 Gloucester	Hereford 3/23
4/17 Hereford	Shrewsbury 6/15
8/10 Shrewsbury	Hereford 10/15

'Bulldogs', 'Counties' and '43XXs' were also utilised for assisting duties on northbound North & West expresses. The last 'County' left in 1932.

It was not until 1931 that the first of the 4-6-0s arrived for a permanent allocation, with 'Saint' No.2944 in March and 'Hall' No.5900 in June. From the mid-1930s, the 'Bulldogs' were largely replaced by the two 4-6-0 classes (and to a lesser extent by '43XXs'), and by January 1938 were down to just three examples.

The ex-L&NW shed at Barrs Court was closed on 4th July 1938, its small allocation of engines thereafter using Barton shed. The engines were probably small tender types for the most part, including ex-L&Y 0-6-0s used on the Midland Brecon services, but larger types did visit daily.

Thus, by 1939, the character of the allocation was somewhat more modern. The turns and allocations were:

Class	Passr	Goods	Shnt	Pilot	Spl	Engines
Hall	2	-	-	-	1	4913, 4952, 4974. 4977, 5965
Saint	2	-	-	-	-	2938, 2951, 2980
Bulldog	2	-	-	1	-	3409, 3432, 3454
26XX	-	1	-	-	-	2680
43XX	1	-	-	-	-	5345, 5377, 6352, 6353
2301	-	1	-	-	1	2325, 2471
45XX	-	1	-	-	-	4534
57XX	-	1	-	-	-	3728, 3789, 7707
2021 }	-	-	4	-	-	2024, 2043, 2101, 2118
74XX }						7416
48XX	-	-	-	-	-	4863

The 4-6-0s were primarily again on the Birmingham & South Wales services, and the 'Bulldogs' were mostly seen on Gloucester or Shrewsbury local passenger duties. Modern 0-6-0PTs were now equal in numbers to the old designs, although the demand for shunting and light freight duties was not great.

Wartime saw a rise in allocation for the light freight and shunting turns, with seven '2021s', two '655s' and four '57XXs' at the shed. In addition to branch working, these worked two shunting turns at Barrs Court, three at Worcester Sidings and one at Barton, whilst another tripped variously between Rotherwas, Barrs Court and Barton. Six 'Halls' ran goods turns as well as the usual passenger duties. One of the 'Saints' was usually favoured for the station pilot duty, and doubled as a standby replacement or assisting engine over the N&W route.

A number of 'J25' 0-6-0s from the L&NER had been loaned to the GWR in place of engines on war duties, and up to four of these were to be found at Hereford between 1940 and 1946 though one or two were the norm, often to be found on local freights over the Gloucester branch.

For a period from April 1942, all the 'Halls' except one were transferred away from the shed, which received seven 'Saints' in their place, making ten in all. Although a couple were subsequently transferred away in the later stages of the war, the number was maintained at eight, and it was not until 1949 that the number of 'Halls' approached the 'Saints' (six and seven respectively).

The 'Bulldogs' just clung on at Hereford into the 1950s, with No.3406 being withdrawn from traffic in January 1951; this ended the 43-year association between shed and class.

By January 1953, the numbers of 4-6-0s had reduced, with '43XXs' becoming the dominant tender type.

Hall	4-6-0	6905, 6916, 6984, 6989
Saint	4-6-0	2920, 2937
28XX	2-8-0	3861
43XX	2-6-0	5377, 6326, 6352, 6362, 6395, 7307, 7308, 7314
2251	0-6-0	2249, 2274, 2281, 2286, 3209
7301	0-6-0	2350, 2515, 2541
57XX	0-6-0PT	3789, 4600, 4657, 4677, 5765, 7707 8701, 9619
2021	0-6-0PT	2138, 2144, 2160
74XX	0-6-0PT	7416

LMR
3F	0-6-0	43277, 43491, 43621, 43822

Hereford was a shed where the GWR (and later, Western Region) often seemed to base engines that were in their final years of service, and visits until the 1950s would reveal '2301s', '2021s' and 'Bulldogs'. Here we see Pontypool Road 'Bulldog' No.3453 *Seagull* on shed at Barton on 6th November 1948; she arrived at that shed in December 1939, and remained there until temporarily placed in storage in December 1948. At this time, Hereford itself housed two of the class, with Nos. 3432 and 3454 resident. No.3453 herself spent nine months at Barton until February 1950, whilst No.3406 was allocated there until January 1951, the last of the class to be so.
P.M. ALEXANDER/MILLBROOK HOUSE

One of the prized allocation of 'Saints' – No.2920 *Saint David* – on shed at Hereford in 1950, along with two pannier tanks. The 'Saints' were utilised on semi-fast and local trains mostly, running largely to Cardiff, Worcester and Birmingham, though still with an occasional express at holiday times, or in place of a failed 'Castle'.
D.K. JONES COLLECTION

Hereford shed seemed to have been an acknowledged final resting place for surviving engines of several veteran designs, both tender and tank. One such class in the 1950s was the 'Dean Goods' 0-6-0, and here No.2541 is seen at the shed on 17th May 1952. These engines covered a wide range of duties ranging from stopping passenger services to Gloucester, Worcester and Shrewsbury, to general freight to a variety of destinations. She finally went in June 1954, after which only No.2474 remained at Barton (until October 1954), with one at Chester and two at Oswestry.

R.C. RILEY/THE TRANSPORT TREASURY

Several ex-Lancashire & Yorkshire 0-6-0s were transferred to Hereford by the LMS to work the Hereford to Brecon service. Here, No.52449 is seen against the original stone shed wall on 17th May 1952. The initials 'BR' on the tender were all that remained of the original full title, an unusual portrayal in the days when the 'cycling lion' emblem was becoming the norm.

R.C. RILEY/THE TRANSPORT TREASURY

Of the above, the '2301' class 0-6-0s Nos.2350 and 2515 were both withdrawn within the following two months, although No.2474 was taken out of storage in the following August to operate at Hereford until October 1954; this was the last engine of the class to be allocated to the shed, No.2541 having gone in June of that year.

At this time, the scheduled 'Saint' turn was to Cardiff, and the three 'Halls' to Birmingham or Worcester. The '43XXs' also had three daily passenger duties to Newport and Cardiff, one to Worcester and one to Gloucester. They were also involved in North & West duties to the south (via Gloucester) when the Severn Tunnel was closed for maintenance on Sundays.

In the summer schedules of 1956, the shed was involved in many passenger duties on all the surrounding lines, and those surviving details may be summarised thus:

Turn	Engine	Working
HFD 1	Hall	Birmingham
HFD 2	43XX	Newport, Cheltenham
HFD 3	43XX	Worcester, Cardiff

HFD 4	Hall	Shrewsbury, Plymouth, Cardiff, Birmingham (Fridays to Sundays)
HFD 5	22XX	Gloucester (2 trips)
HFD 6	22XX	Gloucester
HFD 7	Hall	Birmingham, Cardiff
HFD 8	Hall	Pontypool Rd, Worcester, Cardiff
HFD 15	Manor	Cardiff, Worcester
HFD 16	Hall	Birmingham (2 trips)
HFD 18	Hall	Birmingham
HFD 19	22XX	Cheltenham, Gloucester (2 trips)
HFD 21	Hall	Worcester (2 trips)
HFD 22	Hall	Pontypool Rd, Shrewsbury

This list is believed to be almost complete, and shows the heavy emphasis on the Birmingham, Worcester & South Wales duties, as well as over the Gloucester branch. Shrewsbury duties were few in comparison, although the 4-6-0 passenger pilot was utilised for failed 'Castles' or 'Halls' over the route.

The 'Manor' in the list above (No.7805) had been transferred to Barton in October 1953, and remained there until June 1958.

Through freight duties were few, and surviving records for the summer of 1956 show the following:

HFD 9 (?)	57XX	(ex-Moorfields) Dowlais (Ammonia Tanks)
HFD 19	22XX	Gloucester (also Passr)
HFD 410	49XX	Pontypool Rd
HFD 419	58XX	Pontrilas
HFD 420	43XX	Pontypool Rd
HFD 421	43XX	Harlescott (Salop)
HFD 424	Cl. 7F	Crewe, Pontypool Rd

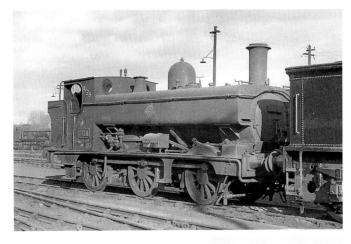

Two members of the '2021' class allocated to Hereford are seen here on shed in the mid-1950s. The class was built at Wolverhampton between 1897 and 1905, and examples had been at Barton since that time, including one out-stationed at Kington. The top picture shows No.2138 standing next to the tender of an L & NW 0-8-0 from either Abergavenny or Shrewsbury depot on 16th October 1955, while the bottom shows the last of the class No.2160 next to an 0-4-2 tank on 15th August 1954. No.2138 was the last of her class to leave Hereford, in May 1956, though one survived at Birkenhead until 1959.   JOHN HODGE

Carlisle Upperby 'Royal Scot' No.46118 *Royal Welch Fusilier* outside the shed after servicing on 18th August 1962. She carried a number code with an 'X', signifying an inter-regional excursion, military or special working. '28XX' 2-8-0 No.3841 alongside was newly-transferred from Severn Tunnel Jct. to Pontypool Road shed. MICHAEL MENSING

LMR 'Royal Scots', 'Jubilees', and '5MT' 4-6-0s could often be found on Hereford shed as here on 21st May 1956 when Longsight's 'Jubilee' No.45638 *Zanzibar* was photographed, having just been coaled, and was now having the long bars put through the fire in preparation for its return working north. They often worked in or out on local passenger duties. JOHN HODGE

The late 1950s saw a reduction in the work at Hereford, with the following turns scheduled for the main engine types for summer 1959:

Class	Turns	Engines
Hall	2	3
43XX	1	3
22XX	4	5
78XXX	1	1
51XX	1	1
42XX	1	2

By the later 1950s, mineral duties in South Wales were beginning to run down, releasing '42XX' class engines for transfer or withdrawal. Barton shed had a pair of '42XXs' from 1955, and a third was added in early 1959, though all had left the shed by early 1960.

Even as late as January 1963, there were still a number of ex-GWR classes represented at the shed, as well as BR Standard designs:

Hall	4-6-0	4907, 4916, 5952, 5970, 5998
2251	0-6-0	2242, 3204 3205
41XX	2-6-2T	4135
57XX	0-6-0PT	3728, 3729, 4623, 4659, 9665
16XX	0-6-0PT	1617, 1657, 1662, 1667
74XX	0-6-0PT	7413
14XX	0-4-2T	1420, 1447
BR		
2MT	2-6-0	78004
3MT	2-6-2T	82001, 82002

By this time, diesels had become the dominant source of power on main line passenger services through Hereford. Meanwhile, the large passenger locomotives remaining were increasingly being utilised for lesser duties than those they had been designed for. Insofar as Hereford was concerned, this involved an allocation of four 'Castles' in October/November 1963 for passenger turns, particularly on the Worcester line; these were to be found on duties previously worked by DMUs. although the arrangement was to be temporary.

The north end of Hereford shed during the 1950s, with '57XX' 0-6-0PT, '28XX' 2-8-0, '2251' 0-6-0 and '51XX' 2-6-2T classes in evidence. Barton shed housed four of the '2251s' in 1951, a figure that rose to nine by mid-1953, though the allocation was reduced to five by 1959 as turns were changed to reflect the demands of traffic.
W.A. CAMWELL

The '56XX' 0-6-2Ts were not engines very frequently seen at Hereford in past years, but one was latterly scheduled to work on the 3.20 p.m. Dowlais to Hereford ammonia tank train (for the Midlands and the North), in this instance No.5661 of Merthyr, on 18th August 1962. She is seen on the road against the west wall of the shed.
MICHAEL MENSING

The coal stage road at Barton shed in April 1964, showing No.7801, an unidentified 'Grange', and '14XXs' Nos.1458 and 1420. Hereford's allocation at this time had shrunk to twenty engines, though including four 'Castles', a couple of '2251s', three '41XXs', the pair of '14XXs' and a mixture of '16XXs' and '57XXs'. Bulmer's cider factory dominates the background to the shed.

R.H. MARROWS

Though not widely seen at Hereford, the '42XXs' did occasionally visit the shed with services from Aberdare, Pontypool Road or Gloucester, and from time to time passing on trains for the Worcester or Shrewsbury routes. However, the shed did acquire two of the class in the latter half of 1955, and they stayed for four or five years. Here, No.5226, which arrived in November 1955, is seen on shed on 5th January 1958; she left Barton in September 1959 for banking work at Bromsgrove.

H.C. CASSERLEY

In January 1964, the shed's duties were:

Class	Type	Passr	Gds	Gds Shnt
Castle	4-6-0	3	-	-
Hall	4-6-0	-	-	-
41XX	2-6-2T	2	-	-
78XXX	2-6-0	-	-	-
32XX	0-6-0	-	2	-
36XX	0-6-0PT	-	-	2
16XX	0-6-0PT	-	2	1
14XX	0-4-2T		1	-

By the summer, the 4-6-0 turns had gone, though the two 2-6-2T duties (now '61XXs') were retained, as were the 0-6-0 ('2251') diagrams, primarily for Gloucester services, with '36XX' and '16XX' on goods or shunting. The '14XX' goods duty was also retained.

The shed ceased operations in December 1964, by which time five 204hp diesel shunter turns on goods (2), passenger (1) and goods shunting (2) were all that remained; these went to Worcester, and Barton shed closed.

Shrewsbury 'Manor' No.7801 *Anthony Manor* is pictured at the coal stage in April 1964, carrying 'H' class lamps, probably having brought a freight into Worcester Sidings or Barton. At this time, only one engine of the class had been withdrawn, and thirteen of the others were to be found at Shrewsbury – and the ex-Cambrian sheds. The stage was of standard design, with two points of delivery for the coal tubs.   R.H. MARROWS

Gloucester 'Mogul' No.6330 crossing onto the Down Goods line, having just come off the Brecon curve out of Worcester Sidings with a short, class 'F' 4.35 p.m. Hereford (Worcester Sidings) to Gloucester goods service on 27th June 1962. The train would spend some forty minutes at Barrs Court Goods before setting off for Rotherwas Jct. and Ross-on-Wye, her next call.
DEREK CROSS

Hereford Brecon Curve signal box, situated in the divergence of the lines to Barrs Court and Barton & Brecon Curve Junctions, is seen here in 1966 with the gates of Burcott Road level crossing in the background.
R.H MARROWS

HEREFORD BARRS COURT NORTH

Oxford 'Hall' No.7900 *Saint Peter's Hall* passing Brecon Curve box on Saturday, 18th September 1954 with what was probably the six-coach 10.10 a.m. Oxford to Hereford express. From 1935, this service was operated by a diesel car (withdrawn for the war years), though from 1948 a passenger train was substituted on Saturdays (and on weekdays during busier periods); doubtless its continued popularity required the full train every day from 1949. The extensive former LNWR/LMS yard is seen on the right and GWR on the left. RUSSELL MULFORD

This section, between Barrs Court Jct. and the passenger station, was originally the preserve of the Shrewsbury & Hereford company, whose joint nature was emphasized by the goods facilities of both the Great Western and London & North Western companies, and by the LNW engine shed. On the east side of the line, a short distance to the south of Barrs Court Jct., was the L&NW engine shed and goods sidings, with their southern boundaries determined by that company's goods shed, which was just to the north of the joint passenger station.

On the opposite (west) side of the running lines was the Great Western's goods yard, again with the southern boundary marked by its goods shed, opposite the L&NW building.

The four running lines were the Up and Down Goods lines (to the east) and Mains (to the west), all of which ran between the two goods sheds on the northern approach to Barrs Court station platforms.

In 1893, the scene was changed significantly by the arrival of the Brecon Curve from the Barton line, with its junction opposite the L&NW engine shed.

Following the closure of the ex-L&NW shed in 1938, the LMS sidings comprised seven at the north end, and three at the south (including the shed road). Between the two were a pair of loops, one of which served the loading dock/cattle pens.

At this time, the Great Western's sidings totalled eleven, with the easternmost serving their goods shed. The company's dock/cattle pens were on the west side of the yard.

The goods loops, which had diverged from the mains just to the north of the L&NW engine shed, were extended northwards in 1941 to provide additional running space for the huge wartime increase in freight movements; their northern junction was now immediately to the north of Barrs Court Jct.

After Nationalisation, the ex-LMS goods shed handled the inwards goods traffic and the ex-GWR depot the outwards, though ultimately all traffic was worked through the ex-GW depot. A zonal

collection and delivery service of goods traffic operated throughout the 1950s, with Hereford depot able to send and receive wagons of smalls (sundries) traffic either direct to and from large depots such as Paddington, Manchester or Liverpool, or to and from other large depots such as Birmingham (Lawley Street), Bristol and Cardiff for transhipment. However, with the introduction of the National Sundries Plan in 1964, Hereford Goods became a Secondary depot under the Cardiff Main depot, and had to send all traffic that could not be loaded direct to Cardiff for transhipment. This provoked an angry reaction from the then depot manager (Mr Neal) as traffic for north of Hereford had to be sent to Cardiff and then came back through Hereford one or two days later, hopefully in direct wagons from Cardiff to a northern destination. Mr Neal maintained that northern traffic should still be sent to Lawley Street for transhipment, but the BRB dictat was otherwise. Fortunately, Cardiff Goods sent a very large number of direct wagons to depots all over the country, and these formed a very useful vacuum head on many long-distance freights from Cardiff Yards.

The removal of goods facilities from the smaller stations had a considerable effect on the Hereford area in the mid-1960s. Where sundries traffic had previously been transhipped at Hereford Goods into/out of wagons to/from Leominster, Woofferton, etc, and delivered or collected by road at those stations, following closure this was all handled direct from Hereford Goods by road.

Following the failure of national replanning to improve the economics and quality of the sundries business, the BRB finally pulled out of this traffic in 1972 and the business passed to private road contractors. Wagon-load traffic was also concentrated at Hereford, making it more difficult and expensive to haul it to or from the outstations, and the BRB pulled out of this traffic, too, in 1976. Thus began the era of the dominance of lorries on the motorways, and the general decline of freight by rail (other than in trainloads), and the virtual elimination of marshalling yards.

During the late morning of Saturday, 18th September 1954, Pontypool Road 'Hall' No.5948 *Siddington Hall* was photographed passing Brecon Curve with the 9.5 a.m. Birkenhead to Cardiff service, numbered '242'. In the summer months, Pontypool Road 'Halls' were employed daily on two or three turns involving North West express or parcels services out to Shrewsbury, Cardiff and Bristol, though on Saturdays that figure could double, with the shed's 'Granges' also utilised.

R. MULFORD

Accelerating away from Barrs Court station with the 3.50 p.m. Hereford to Paddington on 27th June 1962, Worcester 'Castle' No.7011 *Banbury Castle* was carrying the 'A03' boards instead of the scheduled 'A13'. The train comprised the four-coach Hereford portion, which would be added to at Shrub Hill, and would include a dining car. The former L & NW/LMS goods shed is seen to the left of the running lines, and the ex-GW shed to the right, handling the majority of traffic by this time. By the early 1930s, the two companies were working closely together at Hereford (and a few other larger locations) in goods handling, providing a united front against the increasing competition from road transport.

DEREK CROSS

Running along the Up Goods line out of Hereford Barrs Court, Reading 'Hall' No.4915 *Condover Hall* is pictured with a class 'C' express freight, probably running from South Wales to the Midlands, on 27th June 1962. This train was probably conveying tinplate traffic for the car industry in the reinforced vans (from the fourth wagon onwards). These services were largely worked by 'Halls' and 'Granges', which by this time were more common on freight turns than on passenger duties.   DEREK CROSS

The 4.5 p.m. Hereford to Brecon three-coach service pulling away from Barrs Court station on 27th June 1962 behind Brecon '2MT' 2-6-0 No.46518. This train would shortly turn left off the main line to run around the Barton & Brecon Curve, and then swing right at Hay & Brecon Jct. around the Brecon Curve for the line out to Eardisley, Hay-on-Wye, Three Cocks Jct. and Brecon. These trains took around 105 minutes for the picturesque 39¼-mile journey.

164

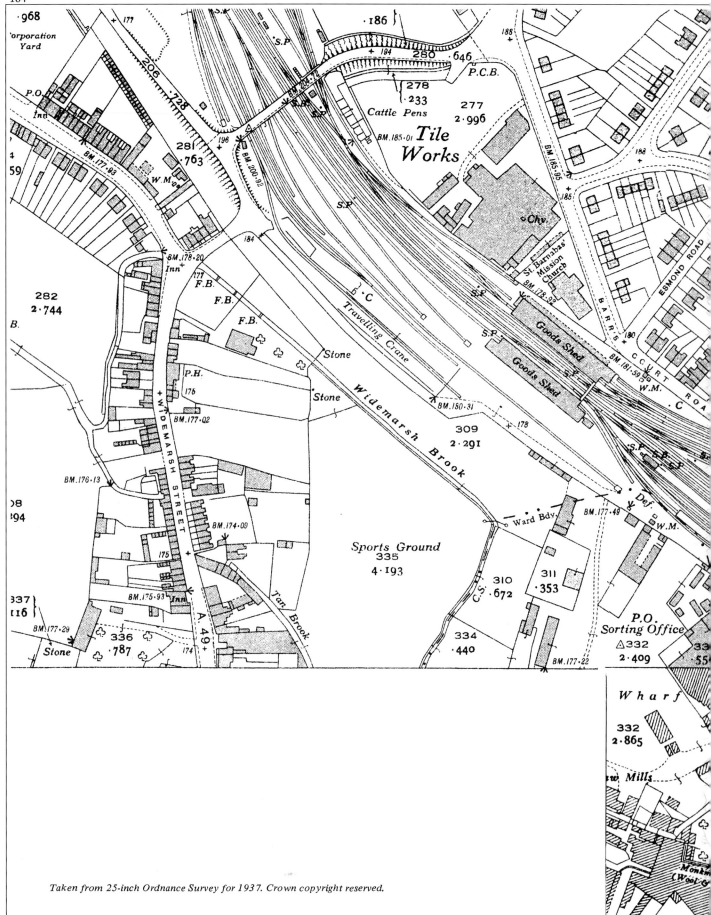

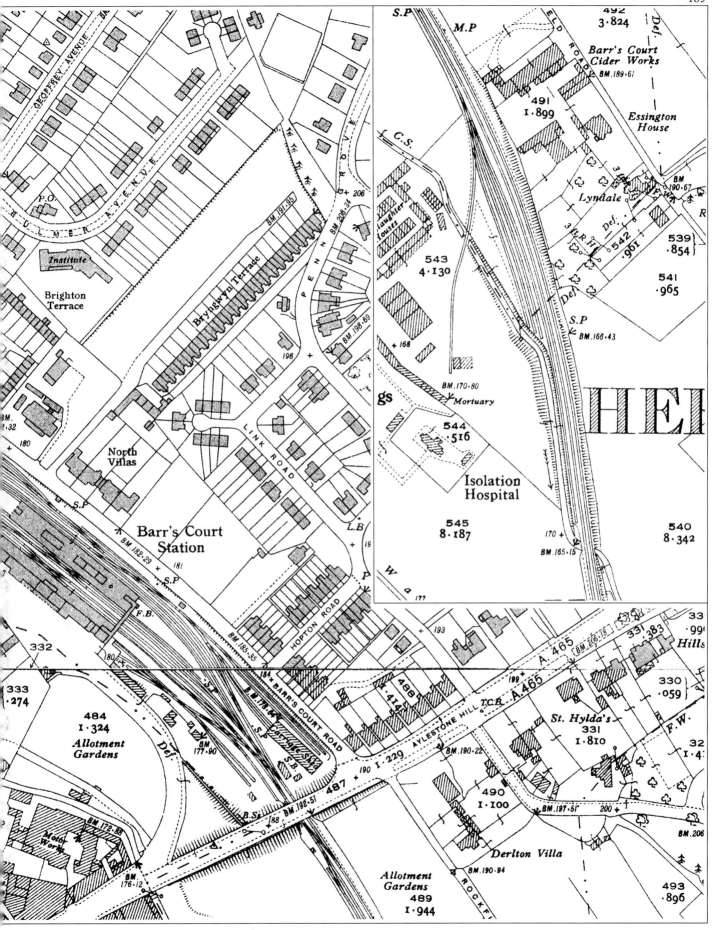

A view looking north from the end of the island platform at Hereford station on 29th April 1960 showing the former GW goods shed on the left and the ex-L & NW shed on the right, with the main lines running between. Hereford '2251' class 0-6-0 No. 2295 is seen on the down goods line through the station with a class 'K' goods service, possibly for the Gloucester line, whilst a 'Hall' was waiting on the up main alongside the ex-GWR goods shed. A train of mixed GWR and Standard Mark 1 stock is seen in the carriage sidings.

R.O. TUCK

A GLIMPSE OF BARRS COURT STATION

The passenger station provided at Barrs Court will be discussed in detail at the beginning of Volume Three of the series, but a brief view of the station is given here to round off the story of the line from Shrewsbury. The station's long history is quite complex, and requires rather more attention than we have room for here. Opened in 1853 in a temporary form, Barrs Court was expanded and rebuilt as other companies became involved, and traffic increased, ending as that imposing structure so well known to travellers on the North & West route.

One of Hereford's stud of three 'Saints' in 1951, No.2944 *Highnam Court*, standing at platform No.2 with an up express. Though the Hereford engines were rostered largely on the Cardiff, Worcester, Birmingham or Shrewsbury trains, they were occasionally seen further afield: in the previous August, No.2944 was recorded at Plymouth, assisting trains over the South Devon banks, doubtless having previously worked a North & West train to Newton.   C.R.L. COLES

Hereford's '2251' class 0-6-0 No.2286 standing at Platform No.3 (old No.2) with the 12.25 p.m. from Gloucester on Saturday, 8th June 1963. The eight Gloucester branch passenger trains were, by now, worked by engines from the sheds at each end of the line, although 1950s services had also seen Swindon and Shrewsbury locomotives on a daily basis. The coach sets working over this route were mostly formed of corridor stock – Brake Compo, Second and Van Second (four sets) – though one four- (7.0 a.m. Hereford) and one five-coach (7.58 a.m. Hereford) formations were also operating daily. The second view shows No.2286 propelling the stock of the 12.25 p.m. Gloucester between the up and down middle lines to await the return working, the 4.30 p.m. to Gloucester.
R.E. TOOP